T. S. Eliot's *The Cocktail Party*

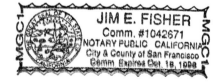

Edited by Nevill Coghill

A CHOICE OF CHAUCER'S VERSE
THE FAMILY REUNION by T. S. Eliot
MURDER IN THE CATHEDRAL by T. S. Eliot

T. S. Eliot's
The Cocktail Party

edited with notes and a commentary by
NEVILL COGHILL

FABER AND FABER LTD
3 Queen Square, London

This edition first published in 1974
by Faber and Faber Limited
3 Queen Square, London W.C.1
Printed in Great Britain by
Robert MacLehose and Company Limited
The University Press, Glasgow
All rights reserved

ISBN 0 571 10472 X (Paper covers)
ISBN 0 571 10592 0 (Hard bound edition)

To Elliot and Henzie Martin Browne

Dear Martin and Henzie,
I would like you to accept the
dedication of this book as a mark of
my admiration for the work you have
both done, on the stage and in the study,
to enrich our understanding and delight
in the plays of T. S. Eliot.
                    Yours affectionately
                        Nevill Coghill

Contents

(*An asterisk in the text signals a note*)

1   *The Cocktail Party*

I WISH to acknowledge my indebtedness to two critics. To Mr. E. Martin Browne, who was responsible for the first production of this play at the Edinburgh Festival, 1949: for his criticism of the structure, from the first version to the last; for suggestions most of which have been accepted, and which, when accepted, have all been fully justified on the stage. And to Mr. John Hayward, for continuous criticism and correction of vocabulary, idiom and manners. My debt to both of these censors could be understood only by comparison of the successive drafts of this play with the final text.

T. S. E.

November 1949

IN addition to some minor corrections, certain alterations in Act III, based on the experience of the play's production, were made in the fourth impression of the text.

T. S. E.

August 1950

Persons

EDWARD CHAMBERLAYNE
JULIA (MRS. SHUTTLETHWAITE)
CELIA COPLESTONE
ALEXANDER MACCOLGIE GIBBS
PETER QUILPE
AN UNIDENTIFIED GUEST, *later identified as*
　　SIR HENRY HARCOURT-REILLY
LAVINIA CHAMBERLAYNE
A NURSE-SECRETARY
TWO CATERER'S MEN

The scene is laid in London

Act One. Scene 1

The drawing-room of the Chamberlaynes' London flat. Early evening. EDWARD CHAMBERLAYNE, JULIA SHUTTLETHWAITE, CELIA COPLESTONE, PETER QUILPE, ALEXANDER MACCOLGIE GIBBS, *and an* UNIDENTIFIED GUEST.

ALEX

You've missed the point completely, Julia:
There *were* no tigers. *That* was the point.

JULIA

Then what were you doing, up in a tree:
You and the Maharaja?

ALEX

My dear Julia!
It's perfectly hopeless. You haven't been listening.

PETER

You'll have to tell us all over again, Alex.

ALEX

I never tell the same story twice.

JULIA

But I'm still waiting to know what happened.
I know it started as a story about tigers.

ALEX

10   I said there were no tigers.

CELIA

Oh do stop wrangling,

Both of you. It's your turn, Julia.

Do tell us that story you told the other day, about Lady
    Klootz and the wedding cake.

PETER

And how the butler found her in the pantry, rinsing her
    mouth out with champagne.

I like that story.*

CELIA

I love that story.

ALEX

I'm never tired of hearing that story.

JULIA

Well, you all seem to know it.

CELIA

Do we all know it?

But we're never tired of hearing *you* tell it.

I don't believe everyone here knows it.
            [*To the* UNIDENTIFIED GUEST]

You don't know it, do you?

UNIDENTIFIED GUEST

No, I've never heard it.

CELIA

Here's one new listener for you, Julia;
And I don't believe that Edward knows it.   20

EDWARD

I may have heard it, but I don't remember it.

CELIA

And Julia's the only person to tell it.
She's such a good mimic.

JULIA

Am I a good mimic?

PETER

You *are* a good mimic. You never miss anything.

ALEX

She never misses anything unless she wants to.

CELIA

Especially the Lithuanian accent.

JULIA

Lithuanian? Lady Klootz?

PETER

I thought she was Belgian.

ALEX

Her father belonged to a Baltic family —
One of the *oldest* Baltic families
With a branch in Sweden and one in Denmark.   30
There were several very lovely daughters:
I wonder what's become of them now.

JULIA

Lady Klootz was very lovely, once upon a time.
What a life she led! I used to say to her: 'Greta!
You have too much vitality.' But she enjoyed herself.
                    [*To the* UNIDENTIFIED GUEST]
Did *you* know Lady Klootz?

                    UNIDENTIFIED GUEST
                            No, I never met her.

                    CELIA

Go on with the story about the wedding cake.

                    JULIA

Well, but it really isn't my story.
I heard it first from Delia Verinder
40 Who was there when it happened.

                    [*To the* UNIDENTIFIED GUEST]
                            Do *you* know Delia Verinder?

                    UNIDENTIFIED GUEST
No, I don't know her.

                    JULIA
                            Well, one can't be too careful
Before one tells a story.

                    ALEX
                    Delia Verinder?
Was she the one who had three brothers?

                    JULIA
How many brothers? Two, I think.

18

ALEX
No, there were three, but you wouldn't know the third one:
They kept him rather quiet.

JULIA
Oh, you mean *that* one.

ALEX
He was feeble-minded.

JULIA
Oh, not feeble-minded:
He was only harmless.

ALEX
Well then, harmless.

JULIA
He was very clever at repairing clocks;
And he had a remarkable sense of hearing —   50
The only man I ever met who could hear the cry of bats.

PETER
Hear the cry of bats?

JULIA
He could hear the cry of bats.

CELIA
But how do you know he could hear the cry of bats?

JULIA
Because he said so. And I believed him.

CELIA

But if he was so . . . harmless, how could you believe him?
He might have imagined it.

JULIA

       My darling Celia,
You needn't be so sceptical. I stayed there once
At their castle in the North. How he suffered!
They had to find an island for him
60 Where there were no bats.

ALEX

       And is he still there?
Julia is really a mine of information.

CELIA

There isn't much that Julia doesn't know.

PETER

Go on with the story about the wedding cake.
          [EDWARD *leaves the room*]

JULIA

No, we'll wait until Edward comes back into the room.
Now I want to relax. Are there any more cocktails?

PETER

But do go on. Edward wasn't listening anyway.

JULIA

No, he wasn't listening, but he's such a strain —
Edward without Lavinia! He's quite impossible!
Leaving it to me to keep things going.
70 What a host! And nothing fit to eat!
The only reason for a cocktail party

For a gluttonous old woman like me
Is a really nice tit-bit. I can drink at home.

[EDWARD *returns with a tray*]
Edward, give me another of those delicious olives.
What's that? Potato crisps? No, I can't endure them.
Well, I started to tell you about Lady Klootz.
It was at the Vincewell wedding. Oh, so many years ago!

[*To the* UNIDENTIFIED GUEST]
Did *you* know the Vincewells?

UNIDENTIFIED GUEST
No, I don't know the Vincewells.

JULIA
Oh, they're both dead now. But I wanted to know.
If they'd been friends of yours, I couldn't tell the story.   80

PETER
Were they the parents of Tony Vincewell?

JULIA
Yes. Tony was the product, but not the solution.
He only made the situation more difficult.
You know Tony Vincewell? You knew him at Oxford?

PETER
No, I never knew him at Oxford:
I came across him last year in California.

JULIA
I've always wanted to go to California.
Do tell us what you were doing in California.

21

CELIA

Making a film.

PETER

Trying to make a film.

JULIA

90 Oh, what film was it? I wonder if I've seen it.

PETER

No, you wouldn't have seen it. As a matter of fact
It was never produced. They did a film
But they used a different scenario.

JULIA

Not the one you wrote?

PETER

Not the one I wrote:
But I had a very enjoyable time.

CELIA

Go on with the story about the wedding cake.

JULIA

Edward, do sit down for a moment.
I know you're always the perfect host,
But just try to pretend you're another guest
100 At Lavinia's party. There are so many questions
I want to ask you. It's a golden opportunity
Now Lavinia's away. I've always said:
'If I could only get Edward alone
And have a really *serious* conversation!'
I said so to Lavinia. She agreed with me.

22

She said: 'I wish you'd try.' And this is the first time
I've ever seen you without Lavinia
Except for the time she got locked in the lavatory
And couldn't get out. I know what you're thinking!
I know you think I'm a silly old woman   110
But I'm really very serious. Lavinia takes me seriously.
I believe that's the reason why she went away —
So that I could make you talk. Perhaps she's in the pantry
Listening to all we say!

EDWARD
No, she's not in the pantry.

CELIA
Will she be away for some time, Edward?

EDWARD
I really don't know until I hear from her.
If her aunt is very ill, she may be gone some time.

CELIA
And how will you manage while she is away?

EDWARD
I really don't know. I may go away myself.

CELIA
Go away yourself!*   120

JULIA
Have you an aunt too?

EDWARD
No, I haven't any aunt. But I might go away.

23

CELIA

But, Edward . . . what was I going to say?
It's dreadful for old ladies alone in the country,
And almost impossible to get a nurse.

JULIA

Is that her Aunt Laura?

EDWARD
                    No; another aunt
Whom you wouldn't know. Her mother's sister
And rather a recluse.

JULIA
                Her favourite aunt?

EDWARD

Her aunt's favourite niece. And she's rather difficult.
When she's ill, she insists on having Lavinia.

JULIA

130 I never heard of her being ill before.

EDWARD

No, she's always very strong. That's why when she's ill
She gets into a panic.

JULIA
                And sends for Lavinia.
I quite understand. Are there any prospects?*

EDWARD

No, I think she put it all into an annuity.

24

JULIA

So it's very unselfish of Lavinia
Yet very like her. But really, Edward,
Lavinia may be away for weeks,
Or she may come back and be called away again.
I understand these tough old women —
I'm one myself. I feel as if I knew   140
All about that aunt in Hampshire.

EDWARD
                         Hampshire?

JULIA

Didn't you say Hampshire?

EDWARD
                    No, I didn't say Hampshire.

JULIA

Did you say Hampstead?

EDWARD
No, I didn't say Hampstead.

JULIA

But she must live somewhere.

EDWARD
                    She lives in Essex.

JULIA

Anywhere near Colchester? Lavinia loves oysters.

EDWARD
No. In the *depths* of Essex.

25

JULIA

Well, we won't probe into it.
You have the address, and the telephone number?
I might run down and see Lavinia
On my way to Cornwall. But let's be sensible:
150   Now you must let me be *your* maiden aunt —
Living on an annuity, of course.
I am going to make you dine alone with me
On Friday, and talk to me about everything.

EDWARD

Everything?

JULIA

Oh, you know what I mean.
The next election. And the secrets of your cases.

EDWARD

Most of my secrets are quite uninteresting.

JULIA

Well, you shan't escape. You dine with me on Friday.
I've already chosen the people you're to meet.

EDWARD

But you asked me to dine with you alone.

JULIA

Yes, alone!
160   Without Lavinia! You'll like the other people —
But you're to talk to me. So that's all settled.
And now I must be going.

EDWARD

Must you be going?

PETER

But won't you tell the story about Lady Klootz?

JULIA

What Lady Klootz?

CELIA

And the wedding cake.

JULIA

Wedding cake? I wasn't at her wedding.
Edward, it's been a delightful evening:
The potato crisps were really excellent.
Now let me see. Have I got everything?
It's such a nice party, I hate to leave it.
It's such a nice party, I'd like to repeat it.   170
Why don't you *all* come to dinner on Friday?
No, I'm afraid my good Mrs. Batten
Would give me notice. And now I must be going.

ALEX

I'm afraid *I* ought to be going.

PETER
Celia —

May I walk along with you?

CELIA
No, I'm sorry, Peter;

I've got to take a taxi.

JULIA
You come with me, Peter:

You can get *me* a taxi, and then I can drop you.

27

I expect you on Friday, Edward. And Celia —
I must see you very soon. Now don't all go
180 Just because I'm going. Good-bye, Edward.

EDWARD

Good-bye, Julia.

[*Exeunt* JULIA *and* PETER]

CELIA
Good-bye, Edward.
Shall I see you soon?

EDWARD
Perhaps. I don't know.

CELIA
Perhaps you don't know? Very well, good-bye.

EDWARD

Good-bye, Celia.

ALEX
Good-bye, Edward. I do hope
You'll have better news of Lavinia's aunt.

EDWARD
Oh . . . yes . . . thank you. Good-bye, Alex,
It was nice of you to come.

[*Exeunt* ALEX *and* CELIA]
[*To the* UNIDENTIFIED GUEST]
Don't go yet.
Don't go yet. We'll finish the cocktails.
Or would you rather have whisky?

UNIDENTIFIED GUEST
Gin.

EDWARD

Anything in it?   190

UNIDENTIFIED GUEST
A drop of water.

EDWARD

I want to apologise for this evening.
The fact is, I tried to put off this party:
These were only the people I couldn't put off
Because I couldn't get at them in time;
And I didn't know that *you* were coming.
I thought that Lavinia had told me the names
Of all the people she said she'd invited.
But it's only that dreadful old woman who mattered —
I shouldn't have minded anyone else,

　　[*The doorbell rings.* EDWARD *goes to the door, saying:*]
But she always turns up when she's least wanted.   200
　　　　　　[*Opens the door*]
Julia!
[*Enter* JULIA]

JULIA

　　Edward! How lucky that it's raining!
It made me remember my umbrella,
And there it is! Now what are you two plotting?
How very lucky it was my umbrella,
And not Alexander's — *he's* so inquisitive!
But *I* never poke into other people's business.
Well, good-bye again. I'm off at last.

　　　　　　　　　　　　　　　　[*Exit*]

EDWARD

I'm sorry. I'm afraid I don't know your name.

UNIDENTIFIED GUEST

I ought to be going.

EDWARD

Don't go yet.

210 I very much want to talk to somebody;
And it's easier to talk to a person you don't know.
The fact is, that Lavinia has left me.

UNIDENTIFIED GUEST

Your wife has left you?*

EDWARD

Without warning, of course;
Just when she'd arranged a cocktail party.
She'd gone when I came in, this afternoon.
She left a note to say that she was leaving me;
But I don't know where she's gone.

UNIDENTIFIED GUEST

This is an occasion.*

May I take another drink?

EDWARD

Whisky?

UNIDENTIFIED GUEST

Gin.

EDWARD

Anything in it?

UNIDENTIFIED GUEST
Nothing but water.
And I recommend you the same prescription . . .   220
Let me prepare it for you, if I may . . .
Strong . . . but sip it slowly . . . and drink it sitting down.
Breathe deeply, and adopt a relaxed position.
There we are. Now for a few questions.
How long married?

EDWARD
Five years.

UNIDENTIFIED GUEST
Children?

EDWARD
No.

UNIDENTIFIED GUEST
Then look at the brighter side.
You say you don't know where she's gone?

EDWARD
No, I do not.

UNIDENTIFIED GUEST
Do you know who the man is?

EDWARD
There was no other man —
None that I know of.

UNIDENTIFIED GUEST
Or another woman
Of whom she thought she had cause to be jealous?   230

EDWARD

She had nothing to complain of in my behaviour.

UNIDENTIFIED GUEST

Then no doubt it's all for the best.
With another man, she might have made a mistake
And want to come back to you. If another woman,
She might decide to be forgiving
And gain an advantage. If there's no other woman
And no other man, then the reason may be deeper
And you've ground for hope that she won't come back at all.
If another man, then you'd want to re-marry
240 To prove to the world that somebody wanted you;
If another woman, you might have to marry her —
You might even imagine that you wanted to marry her.

EDWARD

But I want my wife back.

UNIDENTIFIED GUEST

That's the natural reaction.
It's embarrassing, and inconvenient.
It was inconvenient, having to lie about it
Because you can't tell the truth on the telephone.
It will all take time that you can't well spare;
But I put it to you . . .

EDWARD

Don't put it to me.

UNIDENTIFIED GUEST

Then I suggest . . .

EDWARD

And please don't suggest.
250 I have often used these terms in examining witnesses,

So I don't like them. May I put it to *you*?
I know that I invited this conversation:
But I don't know who you are. This is not what I expected.
I only wanted to relieve my mind
By telling someone what I'd been concealing.
I don't think I want to know who you are;
But, at the same time, unless you know my wife
A good deal better than I thought, or unless you know
A good deal more about us than appears —
I think your speculations rather offensive.   260

UNIDENTIFIED GUEST

I know you as well as I know your wife;
And I knew that all you wanted was the luxury
Of an intimate disclosure to a stranger.
Let me, therefore, remain the stranger.
But let me tell you, that to approach the stranger
Is to invite the unexpected, release a new force,
Or let the genie out of the bottle.
It is to start a train of events
Beyond your control. So let me continue.
I will say then, you experience some relief   270
Of which you're not aware. It will come to you slowly:
When you wake in the morning, when you go to bed at
          night,
That you are beginning to enjoy your independence;
Finding your life becoming cosier and cosier
Without the consistent critic, the patient misunderstander
Arranging life a little better than you like it,
Preferring not quite the same friends as yourself,
Or making your friends like her better than you;
And, turning the past over and over,
You'll wonder only that you endured it for so long.   280
And perhaps at times you will feel a little jealous

That she saw it first, and had the courage to break it —
Thus giving herself a permanent advantage.

EDWARD

It might turn out so, yet . . .

UNIDENTIFIED GUEST
                    Are you going to say, you love her?

EDWARD

Why, I thought we took each other for granted.
I never thought I should be any happier*
With another person. Why speak of love?
We were used to each other. So her going away
At a moment's notice, without explanation,
290   Only a note to say that she had gone
And was not coming back — well, I can't understand it.
Nobody likes to be left with a mystery:
It's so . . . unfinished.

UNIDENTIFIED GUEST
                    Yes, it's unfinished;
And nobody likes to be left with a mystery.
But there's more to it than that. There's a loss of personality;
Or rather, you've lost touch with the person
You thought you were. You no longer feel quite human.
You're suddenly reduced to the status of an object —
A living object, but no longer a person.
300   It's always happening, because one is an object
As well as a person. But we forget about it
As quickly as we can. When you've dressed for a party
And are going downstairs, with everything about you
Arranged to support you in the role you have chosen,
Then sometimes, when you come to the bottom step

34

There is one step more than your feet expected
And you come down with a jolt. Just for a moment
You have the experience of being an object
At the mercy of a malevolent staircase.
Or, take a surgical operation.   310
In consultation with the doctor and the surgeon,
In going to bed in the nursing home,
In talking to the matron, you are still the subject,
The centre of reality. But, stretched on the table,
You are a piece of furniture in a repair shop
For those who surround you, the masked actors;
All there is of you is your body
And the 'you' is withdrawn. May I replenish?

EDWARD
Oh, I'm sorry. What were you drinking?
Whisky?   320

UNIDENTIFIED GUEST
Gin.

EDWARD
Anything with it?

UNIDENTIFIED GUEST
Water.

EDWARD
To what does this lead?

UNIDENTIFIED GUEST
To finding out
What you really are. What you really feel.

What you really are among other people.
Most of the time we take ourselves for granted,
As we have to, and live on a little knowledge
About ourselves as we were. Who are you now?
You don't know any more than I do,
But rather less. You are nothing but a set*
Of obsolete responses. The one thing to do
330 Is to do nothing. Wait.

EDWARD
Wait!
But waiting is the one thing impossible.
Besides, don't you see that it makes me ridiculous?

UNIDENTIFIED GUEST
It will do you no harm to find yourself ridiculous.
Resign yourself to be the fool you are.
That's the best advice that *I* can give you.

EDWARD
But how can I wait, not knowing what I'm waiting for?
Shall I say to my friends, 'My wife has gone away'?
And they answer 'Where?' and I say 'I don't know';
And they say, 'But when will she be back?'
340 And I reply 'I don't know that she *is* coming back'.
And they ask 'But what are you going to do?'
And I answer 'Nothing'. They will think me mad
Or simply contemptible.

UNIDENTIFIED GUEST
All to the good.
You will find that you survive humiliation.
And that's an experience of incalculable value.

EDWARD

Stop! I agree that much of what you've said
Is true enough. But that is not all.
Since I saw her this morning when we had breakfast
I no longer remember what my wife is like.
I am not quite sure that I could describe her   350
If I had to ask the police to search for her.
I'm sure I don't know what she was wearing
When I saw her last. And yet I want her back.
And I *must* get her back, to find out what has happened
During the five years that we've been married.
I must find out who she is, to find out who I am.
And what is the use of all your analysis
If I am to remain always lost in the dark?

UNIDENTIFIED GUEST

There is certainly no purpose in remaining in the dark
Except long enough to clear from the mind   360
The illusion of having ever been in the light.
The fact that you can't give a reason for wanting her
Is the best reason for believing that you want her.

EDWARD

I want to see her again — here.

UNIDENTIFIED GUEST

You shall see her again — here.

EDWARD

Do you mean to say that you know where she is?

UNIDENTIFIED GUEST

That question is not worth the trouble of an answer.
But if I bring her back it must be on one condition:

That you promise to ask her no questions
Of where she has been.

EDWARD
I will not ask them.
370 And yet — it seems to me — when we began to talk
I was not sure I wanted her; and now I want her.
Do I want her? Or is it merely your suggestion?

UNIDENTIFIED GUEST
We do not know yet. In twenty-four hours
She will come to you here. You will be here to meet her.
[*The doorbell rings*]

EDWARD
I must answer the door.
[EDWARD *goes to the door*]
So it's you again, Julia!
[*Enter* JULIA *and* PETER]

JULIA
Edward, I'm so glad to find you.
Do you know, I must have left my glasses here,
And I simply can't see a thing without them.
I've been dragging Peter all over town
380 Looking for them everywhere I've been.
Has anybody found them? You can tell if they're mine —
Some kind of a plastic sort of frame —
I'm afraid I don't remember the colour,
But I'd know them, because one lens is missing.*

UNIDENTIFIED GUEST [*Sings*]
As I was drinkin' gin and water,
And me bein' the One Eyed Riley,

38

> *Who came in but the landlord's daughter*
> *And she took my heart entirely.*

You will keep our appointment?

EDWARD
        I shall keep it.

UNIDENTIFIED GUEST [*Sings*]
    Tooryooly toory-iley,   390
        What's the matter with One Eyed Riley?
                                            [*Exit*]

JULIA
Edward, who *is* that dreadful man?
I've never been so insulted in my life.
It's very lucky that I left my spectacles:
This is what I call an adventure!
Tell me about him. You've been *drinking* together!
So this is the kind of friend you have
When Lavinia is out of the way! Who is he?

EDWARD
I don't know.

JULIA
You don't know?

EDWARD
        I never saw him before in my life.

JULIA
But how did he come here?   400

39

EDWARD
I don't know.

JULIA
You don't know! And what's his name?
Did I hear him say his name was Riley?

EDWARD
I don't know his name.

JULIA
You don't know his *name*?

EDWARD
I tell you I've no idea who he is
Or how he got here.

JULIA
But what did you talk about
Or were you singing songs all the time?
There's altogether too much mystery
About this place to-day.

EDWARD
I'm very sorry.

JULIA
No, I love it. But that reminds me
410 About my glasses. That's the greatest mystery.
Peter! Why aren't you looking for them?
Look on the mantelpiece. Where was I sitting?
Just turn out the bottom of that sofa —
No, this chair. Look under the cushion.

40

EDWARD

Are you quite sure they're not in your bag?

JULIA

Why no, of course not: that's where I keep them.
Oh, here they are! Thank you, Edward;
That really was very clever of you;
I'd never have found them but for you.
The next time I lose *anything*, Edward,   420
I'll come straight to you, instead of to St. Anthony.*
And now I must fly. I've kept the taxi waiting.
Come along, Peter.

PETER

I hope you won't mind
If I don't come with you, Julia? On the way back
I remembered something I had to say to Edward . . .

JULIA

Oh, about Lavinia?

PETER

No, not about Lavinia.
It's something I want to consult him about,
And I could do it now.

JULIA

Of course I don't mind.

PETER

Well, at least you must let me take you down in the lift.

JULIA

No, you stop and talk to Edward. I'm not helpless yet.   430
And besides, I like to manage the machine myself —

In a lift I can meditate. Good-bye then.
And thank you — both of you — very much.

[*Exit*]

PETER

I hope I'm not disturbing you, Edward.

EDWARD

I seem to have been disturbed already;
And I did rather want to be alone.
But what's it all about?

PETER

I want your help.
I was going to telephone and try to see you later;
But this seemed an opportunity.

EDWARD

And what's your trouble?

PETER

440 This evening I felt I could bear it no longer.
That awful party! I'm sorry, Edward;
Of course it was really a very nice party
For everyone but me. And that wasn't your fault.
I don't suppose you noticed the situation.

EDWARD

I did think I noticed one or two things;
But I don't pretend I was aware of everything.

PETER

Oh, I'm very glad that you didn't notice:
I must have behaved rather better than I thought.

42

If you didn't notice, I don't suppose the others did,
Though I'm rather afraid of Julia Shuttlethwaite.   450

EDWARD

Julia is certainly observant,
But I think she had some other matter on her mind.

PETER

It's about Celia. Myself and Celia.

EDWARD

Why, what could there be about yourself and Celia?
Have you anything in common, do you think?

PETER

It seemed to me we had a great deal in common.
We're both of us artists.

EDWARD
I never thought of that.
What arts do you practise?

PETER
You won't have seen my novel,
Though it had some very good reviews.
But it's more the cinema that interests both of us.   460

EDWARD

A common interest in the moving pictures
Frequently brings young people together.

PETER

Now you're only being sarcastic:
Celia was interested in the art of the film.

EDWARD

As a possible profession?

PETER

She might make it a profession;
Though she had her poetry.

EDWARD

Yes, I've seen her poetry —
Interesting if one is interested in Celia.
Apart, of course, from its literary merit
Which I don't pretend to judge.

PETER

Well, I can judge it,
470 And I think it's very good. But that's not the point.
The point is, I thought we had a great deal in common
And I think she thought so too.

EDWARD

How did you come to know her?

[*Enter* ALEX]

ALEX

Ah, there you are, Edward! Do you know why *I*'ve looked
in?

EDWARD

I'd like to know first how you *got* in, Alex.

ALEX

Why, I came and found that the door was open
And so I thought I'd slip in and see if anyone was with you.

PETER
Julia must have left it open.

EDWARD
Never mind;
So long as you both shut it when you go out.

ALEX
Ah, but you're coming with me, Edward.
I thought, Edward may be all alone this evening,   480
And I know that he hates to spend an evening alone,
So you're going to come out and have dinner with me.

EDWARD
That's very thoughtful of you, Alex, I'm sure;
But I rather *want* to be alone, this evening.

ALEX
But you've got to have some dinner. Are you going out?
Is there anyone here to get dinner for you?

EDWARD
No, I shan't want much, and I'll get it myself.

ALEX
Ah, in that case I know what I'll do.
I'm going to give you a little surprise:
You know, I'm rather a famous cook.   490
I'm going straight to your kitchen now
And I shall prepare you a nice little dinner
Which you can have alone. And then we'll leave you.
Meanwhile, you and Peter can go on talking
And I shan't disturb you.

EDWARD
My dear Alex,
There'll be nothing in the larder worthy of your cooking.
I couldn't think of it.

ALEX
                    Ah, but that's my special gift —
Concocting a toothsome meal out of nothing.
Any scraps you have will do. I learned that in the East.
500 With a handful of rice and a little dried fish
I can make half a dozen dishes. Don't say a word.
I shall begin at once.

                              [*Exit to kitchen*]

EDWARD
Well, where did you leave off?

PETER
You asked me how I came to know Celia.
I met her here, about a year ago.

EDWARD
At one of Lavinia's amateur Thursdays?

PETER
A Thursday. Why do you say amateur?

EDWARD
Lavinia's attempts at starting a salon,*
Where I entertained the minor guests
And dealt with the misfits, Lavinia's mistakes.
510 But you were one of the minor successes
For a time at least.

46

PETER

I wouldn't say that.
But Lavinia was awfully kind to me
And I owe her a great deal. And then I met Celia.
She was different from any girl I'd ever known
And not easy to talk to, on that occasion.

EDWARD

Did you see her often?

ALEX'S VOICE

Edward, have you a double boiler?

EDWARD

I suppose there must be a double boiler:
Isn't there one in every kitchen?

ALEX'S VOICE

I can't find it.
There goes *that* surprise. I must think of another.

PETER

Not very often.
And when I did, I got no chance to talk to her.   520

EDWARD

You and Celia were asked for different purposes.
Your role was to be one of Lavinia's discoveries;
Celia's, to provide society and fashion.
Lavinia always had the ambition
To establish herself in two worlds at once —
But she herself had to be the link between them.
That is why, I think, her Thursdays were a failure.

47

PETER

You speak as if everything was finished.

EDWARD

Oh no, no, everything is left unfinished.
530 But you haven't told me how you came to know Celia.

PETER

I saw her again a few days later
Alone at a concert. And I was alone.
I've always gone to concerts alone —
At first, because I knew no one to go with,
And later, I found I preferred to go alone.
But a girl like Celia, it seemed very strange,
Because I had thought of her merely as a name
In a society column, to find her there alone.
Anyway, we got into conversation
540 And I found that she went to concerts alone
And to look at pictures. So we often met
In the same way, and sometimes went together.
And to be with Celia, that was something different
From company or solitude. And we sometimes had tea
And once or twice dined together.

EDWARD

                    And after that
Did she ever introduce you to her family
Or to any of her friends?

PETER

                    No, but once or twice she spoke of them
And about their lack of intellectual interests.

EDWARD

And what happened after that?

48

PETER
                    Oh, nothing happened.
But I thought that she really cared about me.   550
And I was so happy when we were together —
So . . . contented, so . . . at peace: I can't express it;
I had never imagined such quiet happiness.
I had only experienced excitement, delirium,
Desire for possession. It was not like that at all.
It was something very strange. There was such . . .
      tranquillity . . .

EDWARD
And what interrupted this interesting affair?
[*Enter* ALEX *in shirtsleeves and an apron*]

ALEX
Edward, I can't find any curry powder.

EDWARD
There isn't any curry powder. Lavinia hates curry.

ALEX
There goes another surprise, then. I must think.   560
I didn't expect to find any mangoes,
But I *did* count upon curry powder.

                                              [*Exit*]

PETER
That is exactly what I want to know.
She has simply faded — into some other picture —
Like a film effect. She doesn't want to see me;
Makes excuses, not very plausible,
And when I do see her, she seems preoccupied
With some secret excitement which I cannot share.*

EDWARD

Do you think she has simply lost interest in you?

PETER

570 You put it just wrong. I think of it differently.
It is not her interest in *me* that I miss —
But those moments in which we seemed to share some
    perception,
Some feeling, some indefinable experience
In which we were both unaware of ourselves.
In your terms, perhaps, she's lost interest in me.

EDWARD

That is all very normal. If you could only know
How lucky you are. In a little while
This might have become an ordinary affair
Like any other. As the fever cooled
580 You would have found that she was another woman
And that you were another man. I congratulate you
On a timely escape.

PETER

               I should prefer to be spared
Your congratulations. I had to talk to someone.
And I have been telling you of something real —
My first experience of reality
And perhaps it is the last. And you don't understand.

EDWARD

My dear Peter, I have only been telling you
What would have happened to you with Celia
In another six months' time. There it is.
590 You can take it or leave it.

50

PETER
But what am I to do?

EDWARD
Nothing. Wait. Go back to California.

PETER
But I must see Celia.

EDWARD
Will it be the same Celia?
Better be content with the Celia you remember.
Remember! I say it's already a memory.

PETER
But I must see Celia at least to make her tell me
What has happened, in her terms. Until I know that
I shan't know the truth about even the memory.
Did we really share these interests? Did we really feel the
    same
When we heard certain music? Or looked at certain pictures?
There was something real. But what is the reality . . .   600
        [*The telephone rings*]

EDWARD
Excuse me a moment.*
        [*Into telephone*]
        Hello! . . . I can't talk now . . .
Yes, there is . . . Well then, I'll ring you
As soon as I can.
        [*To* PETER]
        I'm sorry. You were saying?

51

PETER

I was saying, what is the reality
Of experience between two unreal people?
If I can only hold to the memory
I can bear any future. But I must find out
The truth about the past, for the sake of the memory.

EDWARD

There's no memory you can wrap in camphor
610 But the moths will get in. So you want to see Celia.
I don't know why I should be taking all this trouble
To protect you from the fool you are.*
What do you want me to do?

PETER

       See Celia for me.
You knew her in a different way from me
And you are so much older.

EDWARD

       So much older?

PETER

Yes, I'm sure that she would listen to you
As someone disinterested.

EDWARD

Well, I will see Celia.

PETER

Thank you, Edward. It's very good of you.
[*Enter* ALEX, *with his jacket on*]

ALEX

Oh, Edward! I've prepared you such a treat!
I really think that of all my triumphs   620
This is the greatest. To make something out of nothing!
Never, even when travelling in Albania,
Have I made such a supper out of so few materials
As I found in your refrigerator. But of course
I was lucky to find half-a-dozen eggs.

EDWARD

What! You used all those eggs! Lavinia's aunt
Has just sent them from the country.

ALEX

                                    Ah, so the aunt
Really exists. A substantial proof.

EDWARD

No, no . . . I mean, this is another aunt.

ALEX

I understand. The real aunt. But you'll be grateful.   630
There are very few peasants in Montenegro
Who can have the dish that you'll be eating, nowadays.

EDWARD

But what about my breakfast?

ALEX

                                Don't worry about breakfast
All you should want is a cup of black coffee
And a little dry toast. I've left it simmering.
Don't leave it longer than another ten minutes.
Now I'll be going, and I'll take Peter with me.

PETER

Edward, I've taken too much of your time,
And you want to be alone. Give my love to Lavinia
640 When she comes back . . . but, if you don't mind,
I'd rather you didn't tell *her* what I've told you.*

EDWARD

I shall not say anything about it to Lavinia.

PETER

Thank you, Edward. Good night.

EDWARD

                    Good night, Peter,
And good night, Alex. Oh, and if you don't mind,
Please *shut the door after you*, so that it latches.

ALEX

Remember, Edward, not more than ten minutes,
Twenty minutes, and my work will be ruined.
                    [*Exeunt* ALEX *and* PETER]
    [EDWARD *picks up the telephone, and dials a number*.]

EDWARD

Is Miss Celia Coplestone in? . . . How long ago? . . .
No, it doesn't matter.

CURTAIN

Act One. Scene 2

The same room: a quarter of an hour later. EDWARD *is
alone, playing Patience. The doorbell rings, and he goes
to answer it.*

CELIA'S VOICE

Are you alone?
[EDWARD *returns with* CELIA]

EDWARD

Celia! Why have you come back?
I said I would telephone as soon as I could:
And I tried to get you a short while ago.

CELIA

If there had happened to be anyone with you
I was going to say I'd come back for my umbrella. . . .
I must say you don't seem very pleased to see me.
Edward, I understand what has happened
But I could not understand your manner on the telephone.
It did not seem like you. So I felt I must see you.
Tell me it's all right, and then I'll go.   10

EDWARD

But how can you say you understand what has happened?
I don't know what has happened, or what is going to happen;
And to try to understand it, I want to be alone.

CELIA

I should have thought it was perfectly simple.
Lavinia has left you.

EDWARD

Yes, that *was* the situation.
I suppose it was pretty obvious to everyone.

CELIA

It was obvious that the aunt was a pure invention
On the spur of the moment, and not a very good one.
You should have been prepared with something better, for
        Julia;
20 But it doesn't really matter. They will know soon enough.
Doesn't that settle all our difficulties?

EDWARD

It has only brought to light the real difficulties.

CELIA

But surely, these are only temporary.
You know I accepted the situation
Because a divorce would ruin your career;
And we thought that Lavinia would never want to leave you.
Surely you don't hold to that silly convention
That the husband must always be the one to be divorced?
And if she chooses to give *you* the grounds . . .

EDWARD

30 I see. But it is not like that at all.
Lavinia is coming back.

CELIA

Lavinia coming back!
Do you mean to say that she's laid a trap for us?

EDWARD

No. If there is a trap, we are all in the trap,
We have set it for ourselves. But I do not know
What kind of trap it is.

CELIA

Then what has happened?
[*The telephone rings*]

EDWARD

Damn the telephone. I suppose I must answer it.
Hello . . . oh, hello! . . . No. I mean yes, Alex;
Yes, of course . . . it was marvellous.
I've never tasted anything like it . . .
Yes, that's very interesting. But I just wondered   40
Whether it mightn't be rather indigestible? . . .
Oh, no, Alex, don't bring me any cheese;
I've got some cheese . . . No, not Norwegian;
But I don't really want cheese . . . Slipper what?* . . .
Oh, from Jugoslavia . . . prunes and alcohol?
No, really, Alex, I don't want anything.
I'm very tired. Thanks awfully, Alex.
Good night.

CELIA

What on earth was that about?

EDWARD

That was Alex.

CELIA

I know it was Alex.
But what was he talking of?   50

EDWARD
                    I had quite forgotten.
He made his way in, a little while ago,
And insisted on cooking me something for supper;
And he said I must eat it within ten minutes.
I suppose it's still cooking.

CELIA
                    You suppose it's still cooking!
I thought I noticed a peculiar smell:
Of course it's still cooking — or doing *something*.
I must go and investigate.
                    [*Starts to leave the room*]

EDWARD
                    For heaven's sake, don't bother!
                                        [*Exit* CELIA]
Suppose someone came and found you in the kitchen?
[EDWARD *goes over to the table and inspects his game of
    Patience. He moves a card. The doorbell rings repeat-
    edly. Re-enter* CELIA, *in an apron.*]

CELIA
You'd better answer the door, Edward.
60 It's the best thing to do. Don't lose your head.
You see, I really did leave my umbrella;
And I'll say I found you here starving and helpless
And had to do something. Anyway, I'm *staying*
And I'm not going to hide.
                    [*Returns to kitchen. The bell rings again.*
            EDWARD *goes to front door, and is heard to say:*]

                    Julia!
What have you come back for?
[*Enter* JULIA]

58

JULIA
I've had an inspiration!

[*Enter* CELIA *with saucepan*]

CELIA

Edward, it's ruined!

EDWARD
What a good thing.

CELIA

But it's ruined the saucepan too.

EDWARD
And half a dozen eggs:
I wanted one for breakfast. A boiled egg.
It's the only thing I know how to cook.

JULIA
Celia! I see you've had the same inspiration   70
That I had. Edward must be fed.
He's under such a strain. We must keep his strength up.
Edward! Don't you realise how lucky you are
To have *two* Good Samaritans? I never heard of that before.

EDWARD
The man who fell among thieves was luckier than I:
He was left at an inn.*

JULIA
Edward, how ungrateful.
What's in that saucepan?

CELIA
Nobody knows.

EDWARD

It's something that Alex came and prepared for me.
He *would* do it. Three Good Samaritans.
80   I forgot all about it.

JULIA
But you mustn't touch it.

EDWARD
Of course I shan't touch it.

JULIA
My dear, I should have warned you
Anything that Alex makes is absolutely deadly.
I could tell such tales of his poisoning people.
Now, my dear, you give me that apron
And we'll see what I can do. You stay and talk to Edward.

[*Exit* JULIA]

CELIA
But what has happened, Edward? What has happened?

EDWARD
Lavinia is coming back, I think.

CELIA
You think! Don't you know?

EDWARD
No, but I believe it. That man who was here —

CELIA
90   Yes, who was that man? I was rather afraid of him;
He has some sort of power.*

60

EDWARD

        I don't know who he is.
But I had some talk with him, when the rest of you had left,
And he said he would bring Lavinia back, tomorrow.

CELIA

But why should that man want to bring her back —
Unless he is the Devil! I could believe he was.*

EDWARD

Because I asked him to.

CELIA

        Because you asked him to!
Then he *must* be the Devil! He must have bewitched you.
How did he persuade you to want her back?
    [*A popping noise is heard from the kitchen*]

EDWARD

What the devil's that?
[*Re-enter* JULIA, *in apron, with a tray and three glasses*]

JULIA

        I've had an inspiration!
There's nothing in the place fit to eat: 100
I've looked high and low. But I found some champagne —
Only a half-bottle, to be sure,
And of course it isn't chilled. But it's so refreshing;
And I thought, we are all in need of a stimulant
After this disaster. Now I'll propose a health.
Can you guess whose health I'm going to propose?

EDWARD

No, I can't. But I won't drink to Alex's.

JULIA

Oh, it isn't Alex's. Come, I give you
Lavinia's aunt! You might have guessed it.

EDWARD *and* CELIA

110   Lavinia's aunt.

JULIA

Now, the next question
Is, what's to be done. That's very simple.
It's too late, or too early, to go to a restaurant.
You must both come home with me.

EDWARD

No, I'm sorry, Julia.
I'm too tired to go out, and I'm not at all hungry.
I shall have a few biscuits.

JULIA

But you, Celia?
You must come and have a light supper with me —
Something very light.

CELIA

Thank you, Julia.
I think I will, if I may follow you
In about ten minutes? Before I go, there's something
120   I want to say to Edward.

JULIA

About Lavinia?
Well, come on quickly. And take a taxi.
You know, you're looking absolutely famished.
Good night, Edward.

[*Exit* JULIA]

CELIA
Well, how did he persuade you?

EDWARD
How did he persuade me? Did he persuade me?
I have a very clear impression
That he tried to persuade me it was all for the best
That Lavinia had gone; that I ought to be thankful.
And yet, the effect of all his argument
Was to make me see that I wanted her back.

CELIA
That's the Devil's method! So you want Lavinia back!   130
Lavinia! So the one thing you care about
Is to avoid a break — anything unpleasant!
No, it can't be that. I won't think it's that.
I think it is just a moment of surrender
To fatigue. And panic. You can't face the trouble.

EDWARD
No, it is not that. It is not only that.

CELIA
It cannot be simply a question of vanity:
That you think the world will laugh at you
Because your wife has left you for another man?
I shall soon put that right, Edward,   140
When you are free.

EDWARD
No, it is not that.
And all these reasons were suggested to me
By the man I call Riley — though his name is not Riley;
It was just a name in a song he sang . . .

CELIA

He sang you a song about a man named Riley!
Really, Edward, I think you are mad —
I mean, you're on the edge of a nervous breakdown.
Edward, if I go away now
Will you promise me to see a very great doctor
150 Whom I have heard of — and his name *is* Reilly!*

EDWARD

It would need someone greater than the greatest doctor
To cure *this* illness.

CELIA
Edward, if I go now,
Will you assure me that everything is right,
That you do not mean to have Lavinia back
And that you do mean to gain your freedom,
And that everything is all right between us?
That's all that matters. Truly, Edward,
If that is right, everything else will be,
I promise you.

EDWARD
No, Celia.
160 It has been very wonderful, and I'm very grateful,
And I think you are a very rare person.
But it was too late. And I should have known
That it wasn't fair to you.

CELIA
It wasn't fair to *me*!
You can stand there and talk about being fair to *me*!

EDWARD

But for Lavinia leaving, this would never have arisen.
What future had you ever thought there could be?

CELIA

What had I thought that the future could be?
I abandoned the future before we began,
And after that I lived in a present
Where time was meaningless, a private world of *ours*,   170
Where the word 'happiness' had a different meaning
Or so it seemed.

EDWARD
I have heard of that experience.*

CELIA

A dream. I was happy in it till to-day,
And then, when Julia asked about Lavinia
And it came to me that Lavinia had left you
And that you would be free — then I suddenly discovered
That the dream was not enough;* that I wanted something
    more
And I waited, and wanted to run to tell you.
Perhaps the dream was better. It seemed the real reality,
And if this is reality, it is very like a dream.   180
Perhaps it was I who betrayed my own dream*
All the while; and to find I wanted
This world as well as that . . . well, it's humiliating.

EDWARD

There is no reason why you should feel humiliated . . .

CELIA

Oh, don't think that you can humiliate me!

Humiliation — it's something I've done to myself.
I am not sure even that you seem real enough
To humiliate me. I suppose that most women
Would feel degraded to find that a man
190 With whom they thought they had shared something
        wonderful
Had taken them only as a passing diversion.
Oh, I dare say that you deceived yourself;
But that's what it was, no doubt.

EDWARD

I *didn't* take you as a passing diversion!
If you want to speak of passing diversions
How did you take Peter?

CELIA
Peter? Peter who?

EDWARD

Peter Quilpe, who was here this evening. *He* was in a dream
And now he is simply unhappy and bewildered.

CELIA

I simply don't know what you are talking about.
200 Edward, this is really too crude a subterfuge
To justify yourself. There was never anything
Between me and Peter.

EDWARD
Wasn't there? *He* thought so.
He came back this evening to talk to me about it.

CELIA
But this is ridiculous! I never gave Peter

66

Any reason to suppose I cared for him.
I thought he had talent; I saw that he was lonely;
I thought that I could help him. I took him to concerts.
But then, as he came to make more acquaintances,
I found him less interesting, and rather conceited.
But why should we talk about Peter? All that matters   210
Is, that you think you want Lavinia.
And if that is the sort of person you are —
Well, you had better have her.

EDWARD
                    It's not like that.
It is not that I am in love with Lavinia.
I don't think I was ever really in love with her.
If I have ever been in love — and I think that I have —
I have never been in love with anyone but you,
And perhaps I still am. But this can't go on.
It never could have been . . . a permanent thing:
You should have a man . . . nearer your own age.*   220

CELIA
I don't think I care for advice from you, Edward:
You are not entitled to take any interest
Now, in *my* future. I only hope you're competent
To manage your own. But if you are not in love
And never have been in love with Lavinia,
What is it that you want?

EDWARD
                    I am not sure.
The one thing of which I am relatively certain
Is, that only since this morning
I have met myself as a middle-aged man
Beginning to know what it is to feel old.   230

That is the worst moment, when you feel that you have lost
The desire for all that was most desirable,
Before you are contented with what you can desire;
Before you know what is left to be desired;
And you go on wishing that you could desire
What desire has left behind. But you cannot understand.
How could *you* understand what it is to feel old?

CELIA

But I want to understand you.* I could understand.
And, Edward, please believe that whatever happens
240 I shall not loathe you. I shall only feel sorry for you.
It's only myself I am in danger of loathing.
But what will your life be? I cannot bear to think of it.
Oh, Edward! Can you be happy with Lavinia?

EDWARD

No — not happy:* or, if there is any happiness,
Only the happiness of knowing
That the misery does not feed on the ruin of loveliness,
That the tedium is not the residue of ecstasy.*
I see that my life was determined long ago
And that the struggle to escape from it
250 Is only a make-believe, a pretence
That what is, is not, or could be changed.
The self that can say 'I want this — or want that' —
The self that wills — he is a feeble creature;
He has to come to terms in the end
With the obstinate, the tougher self; who does not speak,
Who never talks, who cannot argue;
And who in some men may be the *guardian* —*
But in men like me, the dull, the implacable,
The indomitable spirit of mediocrity.
260 The willing self can contrive the disaster

Of this unwilling partnership — but can only flourish
In submission to the rule of the stronger partner.

CELIA

I am not sure, Edward, that I understand you;
And yet I understand as I never did before.
I think — I believe — you are being yourself
As you never were before, with me.
Twice you have changed since I have been looking at you.*
I looked at your face: and I thought that I knew
And loved every contour; and as I looked
It withered, as if I had unwrapped a mummy.   270
I listened to your voice, that had always thrilled me,
And it became another voice — no, not a voice:
What I heard was only the noise of an insect,
Dry, endless, meaningless, inhuman —
You might have made it by scraping your legs together —
Or however grasshoppers do it. I looked,
And listened for your heart, your blood;
And saw only a beetle the size of a man
With nothing more inside it than what comes out
When you tread on a beetle.   280

EDWARD
                    Perhaps that is what I am.
Tread on me, if you like.

CELIA
                    No, I won't tread on you.
That is not what you are. It is only what was left
Of what I had thought you were. I see another person,
I see you as a person whom I never saw before.
The man I saw before, he was only a projection —*
I see that now — of something that I wanted —

69

No, not *wanted* — something I aspired to —
Something that I desperately wanted to exist.
It must happen somewhere — but what, and where is it?
290   Edward, I see that I was simply making use of you.
And I ask you to forgive me.

EDWARD
You . . . ask me to forgive *you*!

CELIA
Yes, for two things. First . . .
[*The telephone rings*]

EDWARD
Damn the telephone.
I suppose I had better answer it.

CELIA
Yes, better answer it.

EDWARD
Hello! . . . Oh, Julia: what is it now?
Your spectacles again . . . where did you leave them?
Or have we . . . have I got to hunt all over?
Have you looked in your bag? . . . Well, don't snap my head
    off . . .
You're sure, in the kitchen? Beside the champagne bottle?
You're quite sure? . . . Very well, hold on if you like;
300   We . . . I'll look for them.

CELIA
Yes, you look for them.
I shall never go into your kitchen again.
[*Exit* EDWARD. *He returns with the spectacles and a bottle*]

70

EDWARD

She was right for once.

CELIA

She is always right.
But why bring an empty champagne bottle?

EDWARD

It isn't empty. It may be a little flat —
But why did she say that it was a half-bottle?
It's one of my best: and I have no half-bottles.
Well, I hoped that you would drink a final glass with me.

CELIA

What should we drink to?

EDWARD

Whom shall we drink to?

CELIA

To the Guardians.

EDWARD

To the Guardians?

CELIA

To the Guardians. It was you who spoke of guardians.   310
                    [*They drink*]
It may be that even Julia is a guardian.
Perhaps she is *my* guardian. Give me the spectacles.
Good night, Edward.

EDWARD

Good night . . . Celia.

[*Exit* CELIA]

Oh!

[*He snatches up the receiver*]

Hello, Julia! are you there? . . .

Well, I'm awfully sorry to have kept you waiting;

But we . . . I had to hunt for them . . . No, I found them.

. . . Yes, she's bringing them now . . . Good night.

CURTAIN

Act One. Scene 3

The same room: late afternoon of the next day. EDWARD
alone. He goes to answer the doorbell.

EDWARD

Oh . . . good evening.
[*Enter the* UNIDENTIFIED GUEST]

UNIDENTIFIED GUEST
Good evening, Mr. Chamberlayne.

EDWARD

Well. May I offer you some gin and water?

UNIDENTIFIED GUEST

No, thank you. This is a different occasion.

EDWARD

I take it that as you have come alone
You have been unsuccessful.

UNIDENTIFIED GUEST
Not at all.
I have come to remind you — you have made a decision.

EDWARD

Are you thinking that I may have changed my mind?

UNIDENTIFIED GUEST

No. You will not be ready to change your mind
Until you recover from having made a decision.
10   No. I have come to tell you that you will change your mind,
But that it will not matter. It will be too late.

EDWARD

I have half a mind to change my mind now
To show you that I am free to change it.

UNIDENTIFIED GUEST

You will change your mind, but you are not free.
Your moment of freedom was yesterday.
You made a decision. You set in motion
Forces in your life and in the lives of others
Which cannot be reversed. That is one consideration.
And another is this: it is a serious matter
20   To bring someone back from the dead.*

EDWARD

From the dead?
That figure of speech is somewhat . . . dramatic,
As it was only yesterday that my wife left me.

UNIDENTIFIED GUEST

Ah, but we die to each other daily.*
What we know of other people
Is only our memory of the moments
During which we knew them. And they have changed
          since then.
To pretend that they and we are the same
Is a useful and convenient social convention
Which must sometimes be broken. We must also remember
30   That at every meeting we are meeting a stranger.

74

EDWARD

So you want me to greet my wife as a stranger?
That will not be easy.

UNIDENTIFIED GUEST
It is very difficult.

But it is perhaps still more difficult
To keep up the pretence that you are not strangers.
The affectionate ghosts: the grandmother,
The lively bachelor uncle at the Christmas party,
The beloved nursemaid — those who enfolded
Your childhood years in comfort, mirth, security —
If they returned, would it not be embarrassing?
What would you say to them, or they to you   40
After the first ten minutes? You would find it difficult
To treat them as strangers, but still more difficult
To pretend that you were not strange to each other.

EDWARD

You can hardly expect me to obliterate
The last five years.

UNIDENTIFIED GUEST
I ask you to forget nothing.

To try to forget is to try to conceal.

EDWARD

There are certainly things I should like to forget.

UNIDENTIFIED GUEST

And persons also. But you must not forget them.
You must face them all, but meet them as strangers.

EDWARD

Then I myself must also be a stranger.   50

75

UNIDENTIFIED GUEST

And to yourself as well. But remember,
When you see your wife, you must ask no questions
And give no explanations. I have said the same to her.
Don't strangle each other with knotted memories.
Now I shall go.

EDWARD

Stop! Will you come back with her?

UNIDENTIFIED GUEST

No, I shall not come with her.

EDWARD

I don't know why,
But I think I should like you to bring her yourself.

UNIDENTIFIED GUEST

Yes, I know you would. And for definite reasons*
Which I am not prepared to explain to you
60   I must ask you not to speak of me to her;
And she will not mention me to you.

EDWARD

I promise.

UNIDENTIFIED GUEST

And now you must await your visitors.

EDWARD

Visitors? What visitors?

UNIDENTIFIED GUEST

Whoever comes. The strangers.
As for myself, I shall take the precaution
Of leaving by the service staircase.

76

EDWARD

May I ask one question?

UNIDENTIFIED GUEST
You may ask it.

EDWARD

Who are you?

UNIDENTIFIED GUEST
I also am a stranger.
[*Exit. A pause.* EDWARD *moves about restlessly. The bell
rings, and he goes to the front door.*]

EDWARD

Celia!

CELIA
Has Lavinia arrived?

EDWARD
Celia! Why have you come?
I expect Lavinia at any moment.
You must not be here. Why have you come here?   70

CELIA
Because Lavinia asked me.

EDWARD
Because Lavinia asked you!

CELIA
Well, not directly, Julia had a telegram*
Asking her to come, and to bring me with her.
Julia was delayed, and sent me on ahead.

EDWARD

It seems very odd. And not like Lavinia.
I suppose there is nothing to do but wait.
Won't you sit down?

CELIA
Thank you.
[*Pause*]

EDWARD

Oh, my God, what shall we talk about?
We can't sit here in silence.

CELIA
Oh, I could.

80   Just looking at you. Edward, forgive my laughing.
You look like a little boy who's been sent for
To the headmaster's study; and is not quite sure
What he's been found out in. I never saw you so before.
This is really a ludicrous situation.

EDWARD

I'm afraid I can't see the humorous side of it.

CELIA

I'm not really laughing at *you*, Edward.
I couldn't have laughed at anything, yesterday;
But I've learnt a lot in twenty-four hours.
It wasn't a very pleasant experience.
90   Oh, I'm glad I came!
I can see you at last as a human being.
Can't you see me that way too, and laugh about it?*

EDWARD

I wish I could. I wish I understood anything.

78

I'm completely in the dark.

CELIA
But it's all so simple.
Can't you see that . . .
                    [*The doorbell rings*]

EDWARD
There's Lavinia.
[*Goes to front door*]
                              Peter!
[*Enter* PETER]

PETER

Where's Lavinia?

EDWARD
Don't tell me that Lavinia
Sent you a telegram . . .

PETER
No, not to me,
But to Alex. She told him to come here
And to bring me with him. He'll be here in a minute.
Celia! Have you heard from Lavinia too?   100
Or am I interrupting?

CELIA
I've just explained to Edward —
I only got here this moment myself —
That she telegraphed to Julia to come and bring me with her.

EDWARD
I wonder whom else Lavinia has invited.

PETER

Why, I got the impression that Lavinia intended
To have yesterday's cocktail party to-day
So I don't suppose her aunt can have died.

EDWARD

What aunt?

PETER

The aunt you told us about.
But Edward — you remember our conversation yesterday?

EDWARD

110   Of course.

PETER

I hope you've done nothing about it.

EDWARD

No, I've done nothing.

PETER

I'm so glad.
Because I've changed my mind. I mean, I've decided
That it's all no use. I'm going to California.

CELIA

You're going to California!

PETER

Yes, I have a new job.

EDWARD

And how did that happen, overnight?

PETER

Why, it's a man Alex put me in touch with
And we settled everything this morning.
Alex is a wonderful person to know,
Because, you see, he knows everybody, everywhere.
So what I've really come for is to say good-bye.   120

CELIA

Well, Peter, I'm awfully glad, for your sake,
Though of course we . . . I shall miss you;
You know how I depended on you for concerts,
And picture exhibitions — more than you realised.
It *was* fun, wasn't it! But now you'll have a chance,
I hope, to realise your ambitions.
I shall miss you.

PETER

It's nice of you to say so;
But you'll find someone better, to go about with.

CELIA

I don't think that I shall be going to concerts.
I am going away too.   130
    [LAVINIA *lets herself in with a latch-key*]

PETER
You're going abroad?

CELIA

I don't know. Perhaps.

EDWARD
You're both going away!

81

[*Enter* LAVINIA]

LAVINIA
Who's going away? Well, Celia. Well, Peter.
I didn't expect to find either of you here.

PETER *and* CELIA
But the telegram!

LAVINIA
What telegram?

CELIA
The one you sent to Julia.

PETER
And the one you sent to Alex.

LAVINIA
I don't know what you mean.
Edward, have you been sending telegrams?

EDWARD
Of course I haven't sent any telegrams.

LAVINIA
This is some of Julia's mischief.
And is *she* coming?

PETER
Yes, and Alex.

LAVINIA
140 Then I shall ask *them* for an explanation.
Meanwhile, I suppose we might as well sit down.
What shall we talk about?

EDWARD
Peter's going to America.

PETER
Yes, and I would have rung you up tomorrow
And come in to say good-bye before I left.

LAVINIA
And Celia's going too? Was that what I heard?
I congratulate you both. To Hollywood, of course?
How exciting for you, Celia! Now you'll have a chance
At last, to realise your ambitions.
You're going together?

PETER
We're not going together.
Celia told us she was going away,   150
But I don't know where.

LAVINIA
You don't know where?
And do you know where you are going, yourself?

PETER
Yes, of course, I'm going to California.

LAVINIA
Well, Celia, why don't you go to California?
Everyone says it's a wonderful climate:
The people who go there never want to leave it.

CELIA
Lavinia, I think I understand about Peter . . .

LAVINIA

I have no doubt you do.

CELIA
And why he is going . . .

LAVINIA

I don't doubt that either.

CELIA
And I believe he is right to go.

LAVINIA

160 Oh, so you advised him?

PETER
She knew nothing about it.

CELIA

But now that I may be going away — somewhere —
I should like to say good-bye — as friends.

LAVINIA

Why, Celia, but haven't we always been friends?
I thought you were one of my dearest friends —
At least, in so far as a girl *can* be a friend
Of a woman so much older than herself.

CELIA
Lavinia,
Don't put me off. I may not see you again.
What I want to say is this: I should like you to remember me
As someone who wants you and Edward to be happy.

84

LAVINIA

You are very kind, but very mysterious.   170
I am sure that we shall manage somehow, thank you,
As we have in the past.

CELIA

Oh, not as in the past!
[*The doorbell rings, and* EDWARD *goes to answer it*]
Oh, I'm afraid that all this sounds rather silly!
But . . .
[EDWARD *re-enters with* JULIA]

JULIA

There you are, Lavinia! I'm sorry to be late.
But your telegram was a bit unexpected.
I dropped everything to come. And how is the dear aunt?

LAVINIA

So far as I know, she is very well, thank you.

JULIA

She must have made a marvellous recovery.
I said so to myself, when I got your telegram.

LAVINIA

But where, may I ask, was this telegram sent from?   180

JULIA

Why, from Essex, of course.

LAVINIA

And why from Essex?

JULIA

Because you've been in Essex.

LAVINIA
Because I've been in Essex!

JULIA
Lavinia! Don't say you've had a lapse of memory!
Then that accounts for the aunt — and the telegram.

LAVINIA
Well, perhaps I was in Essex. I really don't know.

JULIA
You don't know where you were? Lavinia!
Don't tell me you were abducted! Tell us
I'm thrilled . . .
[*The doorbell rings.* EDWARD *goes to answer it. Enter* ALEX.]

ALEX
Has Lavinia arrived?

EDWARD
Yes.

ALEX
Welcome back, Lavinia!
190   When I got your telegram . . .

LAVINIA
Where from?

ALEX
Dedham.*

LAVINIA
Dedham is in Essex. So it was from Dedham.
Edward, have *you* any friends in Dedham?

86

EDWARD

No, *I* have no connections in Dedham.

JULIA

Well, it's all delightfully mysterious.

ALEX

But what is the mystery?

JULIA

Alex, *don't* be inquisitive.
Lavinia has had a lapse of memory,
And so, of course, she sent us telegrams:
And now I don't believe she really wants us.
I can see that she is quite worn out
After her anxiety about her aunt —   200
Who you'll be glad to hear, has quite recovered, Alex —
And after that long journey on the old Great Eastern,
Waiting at junctions. And I suppose she's famished.

ALEX

Ah, in that case I know what I'll do . . .

JULIA

No, Alex.
We must leave them alone, and let Lavinia rest.
Now we'll all go back to *my* house. Peter, call a taxi.

                                        [*Exit* PETER]

We'll have a cocktail party at *my* house to-day.

CELIA

Well, I'll go now. Good-bye, Lavinia.
Good-bye, Edward.

EDWARD
Good-bye, Celia.

CELIA
210   Good-bye, Lavinia.

LAVINIA
Good-bye, Celia.

[*Exit* CELIA]

JULIA
And now, Alex, you and I should be going.

EDWARD
Are you sure you haven't left anything, Julia?

JULIA
Left anything? Oh, you mean my spectacles.
No, they're here. Besides, they're no use to me.
I'm not coming back again *this* evening.

LAVINIA
Stop! I want you to explain the telegram.

JULIA
Explain the telegram? What do you think, Alex?

ALEX
No, Julia, *we* can't explain the telegram.

LAVINIA
I am sure that you could explain the telegram.
220   I don't know why. But it seems to me that yesterday
I started some machine,* that goes on working,

And I cannot stop it; no, it's not like a machine —
Or if it's a machine, someone else is running it.
But who? Somebody is always interfering* . . .
I don't feel free . . . and yet I started it . . .

JULIA
Alex, do you think we could explain *anything*?

ALEX
I think not, Julia. She must find out for herself:
That's the only way.

JULIA
How right you are!
Well, my dears, I shall see you very soon.

EDWARD
When shall we see you?   230

JULIA
Did I say you'd see me?
Good-bye. I believe . . . I haven't left anything.
[*Enter* PETER]

PETER
I've got a taxi, Julia.

JULIA
Splendid! Good-bye!
                    [*Exeunt* JULIA, ALEX *and* PETER]

LAVINIA
I must say, you don't seem very pleased to see me.

EDWARD

I can't say that I've had much opportunity
To seem anything. But of course I'm glad to see you.

LAVINIA

Yes, that was a silly thing to say.
Like a schoolgirl. Like Celia. I don't know why I said it.
Well, here I am.

EDWARD

I am to ask no questions.

LAVINIA

And I know I am to give no explanations.

EDWARD

240 And I am to give no explanations.

LAVINIA

And I am to ask no questions. And yet . . . why not?

EDWARD

I don't know why not. So what are we to talk about?

LAVINIA

There is one thing I ought to know, because of other people
And what to do about them. It's about that party.
I suppose you won't believe I forgot all about it!
I let you down badly. What did you do about it?
I only remembered after I had left.

EDWARD

I telephoned to everyone I knew was coming
But I couldn't get everyone. And so a few came.

90

LAVINIA

Who came?   250

EDWARD
Just those who were here this evening . . .

LAVINIA

That's odd.

EDWARD
. . . and one other. I don't know who he was,
But *you* ought to know.*

LAVINIA
Yes, I think I know.
But I'm puzzled by Julia. That woman is the devil.
She knows by instinct when something's going to happen.
Trust her not to miss any awkward situation!
And what did you tell them?

EDWARD
I invented an aunt
Who was ill in the country, and had sent for you.

LAVINIA
Really, Edward! You had better have told the truth:
Nothing less that the truth could deceive Julia.
But how did the aunt come to live in Essex?   260

EDWARD
Julia compelled me to make her live somewhere.

LAVINIA
I see. So Julia made her live in Essex;
And made the telegrams come from Essex.

91

Well, I shall have to tell Julia the truth.
I shall always tell the truth now.
We have wasted such a lot of time in lying.

EDWARD

I don't quite know what you mean.

LAVINIA
Oh, Edward!
The point is, that since I've been away
I see that I've taken you much too seriously.
270   And now I can see how absurd you are.*

EDWARD

That is a very serious conclusion
To have arrived at in . . . how many? . . . thirty-two hours.

LAVINIA

Yes, a very important discovery,
Finding that you've spent five years of your life
With a man who has no sense of humour;
And that the effect upon me was
That I lost all sense of humour myself.
That's what came of always giving in to you.

EDWARD

I was unaware that you'd always given in to me.
280   It struck me very differently. As we're on the subject,
I thought that it was I who had given in to *you*.

LAVINIA

I know what you mean by giving in to *me*:
You mean, leaving all the practical decisions
That you should have made yourself. I remember —

Oh, I ought to have realised what was coming —
When we were planning our honeymoon,
I couldn't make you say where you wanted to go . . .

EDWARD

But I wanted *you* to make that decision.

LAVINIA

But how could I tell where I wanted to go
Unless you suggested some other place first?   290
And I remember that finally in desperation
I said : 'I suppose you'd as soon go to Peacehaven' —
And you said 'I don't mind'.

EDWARD
                    Of course I didn't mind.
I meant it as a compliment.

LAVINIA
                    You meant it as a compliment !
And you were so considerate, people said ;
And you thought you were unselfish. It was only passivity ;
You only wanted to be bolstered, encouraged. . . .

EDWARD

Encouraged? To what?

LAVINIA
                    To think well of yourself.
You know it was I who made you work at the Bar . . .

EDWARD

You nagged me because I didn't get enough work   300
And said that I ought to meet more people :

But when the briefs began to come in —
And they didn't come through any of *your* friends —
You suddenly found it inconvenient
That I should be always too busy or too tired
To be of use to you socially . . .

LAVINIA

       I *never* complained.

EDWARD

No; and it was perfectly infuriating,
The way you *didn't* complain . . .

LAVINIA

       It was you who complained
Of seeing nobody but solicitors and clients . . .

EDWARD

310 And you were never very sympathetic.

LAVINIA

Well, I tried to do something about it.
That was why I took so much trouble
To have those Thursdays, to give you the chance
Of talking to intellectual people . . .

EDWARD

You would have given me about as much opportunity
If you had hired me as your butler:
Some of your guests may have thought I *was* the butler.

LAVINIA

And on several occasions, when somebody was coming
Whom I particularly wanted you to meet,
320 You didn't arrive until just as they were leaving.

94

EDWARD

Well, at least, they can't have thought I was the butler.

LAVINIA

Everything I tried only made matters worse,
And the moment you were offered something that you
      wanted
You wanted something else. I shall treat you very differently
In future.

EDWARD

      Thank you for the warning. But tell me,
Since this is how you see me, why did you come back?

LAVINIA

Frankly, I don't know. I was warned of the danger,*
Yet something, or somebody, compelled me to come.
And why did you want me?

EDWARD

      I don't know either.
You say you were trying to 'encourage' me: 330
Then why did you always make me feel insignificant?
I may not have known what life I wanted,
But it wasn't the life you chose for me.
You wanted your husband to be *successful*,
You wanted me to supply a public background
For your kind of public life. You wished to be a hostess
For whom my career would be a support.
Well, I tried to be accommodating. But, in future,
I shall behave, I assure you, very differently.

LAVINIA

Bravo! Edward. This is surprising.   340
Now who could have taught you to answer back like that?

EDWARD

I have had quite enough humiliation
Lately, to bring me to the point
At which humiliation ceases to humiliate.
You get to the point at which you cease to feel
And then you speak your mind.

LAVINIA

      That will be a novelty
To find that you have a mind to speak.
Anyway, I'm prepared to take you as you are.

EDWARD

You mean you are prepared to take me
350 As I was, or as you think I am.
But what do you think I am?

LAVINIA

      Oh, what you always were.
As for me, I'm rather a different person
Whom you must get to know.

EDWARD

      This is very interesting:
But you seem to assume that you've done all the changing —
Though I haven't yet found it a change for the better.
But doesn't it occur to you that possibly
I may have changed too?

LAVINIA

      Oh, Edward, when you were a little boy,*
I'm sure you were always getting yourself measured
To prove how you had grown since the last holidays.
360 You were always intensely concerned with yourself;

And if other people grow, well, you want to grow too.
In what way have you changed?

EDWARD

                    The change that comes
From seeing oneself through the eyes of other people.

LAVINIA

That must have been very shattering for you.
But never mind, you'll soon get over it
And find yourself another little part to play,
With another face, to take people in.

EDWARD

One of the most infuriating things about you
Has always been your perfect assurance
That you understood me better than I understood myself.   370

LAVINIA

And the most infuriating thing about you
Has always been your placid assumption
That I wasn't worth the trouble of understanding.

EDWARD

So here we are again. Back in the trap,
With only one difference, perhaps — we can fight each
    other,
Instead of each taking his corner of the cage.
Well, it's a better way of passing the evening
Than listening to the gramophone.

LAVINIA

                 We have very good records;
But I always suspected that you really hated music

D   97

380 And that the gramophone was only your escape
From talking to me when we had to be alone.

EDWARD

I've often wondered why you married me.

LAVINIA

Well, you really were rather attractive, you know;
And you kept on *saying* that you were in love with me —
I believe you were trying to persuade yourself you were.
I seemed always on the verge of some wonderful experience
And then it never happened. I wonder now
How you could have thought you were in love with me.

EDWARD

Everybody told me that I was;
390 And they told me how well suited we were.

LAVINIA

It's a pity that you had no opinion of your own.
Oh, Edward, I should like to be good to you —
Or if that's impossible, at least be horrid to you —
Anything but nothing, which is all you seem to want of me.
But I'm sorry for you . . .

EDWARD

                    Don't say you are sorry for me!
I have had enough of people being sorry for me.

LAVINIA

Yes, because they can never be so sorry for you
As you are for yourself. And that's hard to bear.
I thought that there might be some way out for you
400 If I went away. I thought that if I died

98

To you, I who had been only a ghost to you,
You might be able to find the road back
To a time when you were real — for you must have been real
At some time or other, before you ever knew me:
Perhaps only when you were a child.

EDWARD

I don't want you to make yourself responsible for me:
It's only another kind of contempt.
And I do not want you to explain me to myself.
You're still trying to invent a personality for me
Which will only keep me away from myself.   410

LAVINIA

You're complicating what is in fact very simple.
But there is one point which I see clearly:
We are not to relapse into the kind of life we led
Until yesterday morning.

EDWARD
There was a door
And I could not open it. I could not touch the handle.
Why could I not walk out of my prison?
What is hell? Hell is oneself,
Hell is alone, the other figures in it
Merely projections.* There is nothing to escape from
And nothing to escape to. One is always alone.   420

LAVINIA

Edward, what *are* you talking about?
Talking to yourself. Could you bear, for a moment,
To think about *me*?

EDWARD

It was only yesterday*
That damnation took place. And now I must live with it
Day by day, hour by hour, for ever and ever.

LAVINIA

I think you're on the edge of a nervous breakdown!

EDWARD

Don't say that!

LAVINIA

I must say it.
I know . . . of a doctor who I think could help you.

EDWARD

If I go to a doctor, I shall make my own choice;
430   Not take one whom you choose. How do I know
That you wouldn't see him first, and tell him all about me
From *your* point of view? But I don't need a doctor.
I am simply in hell. Where there are no doctors —
At least, not in a professional capacity.

LAVINIA

One can be practical, even in hell:
And you know I am much more practical than you are.

EDWARD

I ought to know by now what you consider practical.
Practical! I remember, on our honeymoon,
You were always wrapping things up in tissue paper
440   And then had to unwrap everything again
To find what you wanted. And I could never teach you
How to put the cap on a tube of tooth-paste.

LAVINIA

Very well then, I shall not try to press you.
You're much too divided to know what you want.
But, being divided, you will tend to compromise,
And your sort of compromise will be the old one.

EDWARD

You don't understand me. Have I not made it clear
That in future you will find me a different person?

LAVINIA

Indeed. And has the difference nothing to do
With Celia going to California?   450

EDWARD

Celia? Going to California?

LAVINIA

       Yes, with Peter.*
Really, Edward, if you were human
You would burst out laughing. But you won't.

EDWARD

O God, O God, if I could return to yesterday
Before I thought that I had made a decision.
What devil left the door on the latch
For these doubts to enter? And then you came back, you
The angel of destruction — just as I felt sure.
In a moment, at your touch, there is nothing but ruin.
O God, what have I done? The python. The octopus.   460
Must I become after all what you would make me?

101

LAVINIA

Well, Edward, as I am unable to make you laugh,
And as I can't persuade you to see a doctor,
There's nothing else at present that I can do about it.
I ought to go and have a look in the kitchen.
I know there are some eggs. But we must go out for dinner.
Meanwhile, my luggage is in the hall downstairs:
Will you get the porter to fetch it up for me?

CURTAIN

Act Two

SIR HENRY HARCOURT-REILLY'S *consulting room in London. Morning: several weeks later.* SIR HENRY *alone at his desk. He presses an electric button. The* NURSE-SECRETARY *enters, with Appointment Book.*

REILLY

About those three appointments this morning, Miss
    Barraway:
I should like to run over my instructions again.
You understand, of course, that it is important
To avoid any meeting?

NURSE-SECRETARY

              You made that clear, Sir Henry:
The first appointment at eleven o'clock.
He is to be shown into the small waiting-room;
And you will see him almost at once.

REILLY

I shall see him at once. And the second?

NURSE-SECRETARY

The second to be shown into the other room
Just as usual. She arrives at a quarter past;   10
But you may keep her waiting.

REILLY
                    Or she may keep me waiting;
But I think she will be punctual.

NURSE-SECRETARY
                    I telephone through
The moment she arrives. I leave her there
Until you ring three times.

REILLY
                    And the third patient?

NURSE-SECRETARY
The third one to be shown into the small room;
And I need not let you know that she has arrived.
Then, when you ring, I show the others out;
And only after they have left the house. . . .

REILLY
Quite right, Miss Barraway. That's all for the moment.

NURSE-SECRETARY
20 Mr. Gibbs is here, Sir Henry.

REILLY
                    Ask him to come straight in.
                              [*Exit* NURSE-SECRETARY]
[ALEX *enters almost immediately*]

ALEX
When is Chamberlayne's appointment?

REILLY
                              At eleven o'clock,
The conventional hour. We have not much time.

Tell me now, did you have any difficulty
In convincing him I was the man for his case?

ALEX

Difficulty? No! He was only impatient
At having to wait four days for the appointment.

REILLY

It was necessary to delay his appointment
To lower his resistance. But what I mean is,
Does he trust your judgement?

ALEX

Yes, implicitly.
It's not that he regards me as very intelligent,   30
But he thinks I'm well informed: the sort of person
Who would know the right doctor, as well as the right shops
Besides, he was ready to consult any doctor
Recommended by anyone except his wife.

REILLY

I had already impressed upon her
That she was not to mention my name to him.

ALEX

With your usual foresight. Now, he's quite triumphant
Because he thinks he's stolen a march on her.
And when you've sent him to a sanatorium*
Where she can't get at him — then, he believes,   40
She will be very penitent. He's enjoying his illness.

REILLY

Illness offers him a double advantage:
To escape from himself — and get the better of his wife.

ALEX

Not to escape from her?

REILLY

He doesn't want to escape from her.

ALEX

He is staying at his club.

REILLY

Yes, that is where he wrote from.
[*The house-telephone rings*]
Hello! Yes, show him up.

ALEX

You will have a busy morning!
I will go out by the service staircase
And come back when they've gone.

REILLY

Yes, when they've gone.
[*Exit* ALEX *by side door*]
[EDWARD *is shown in by* NURSE-SECRETARY]

EDWARD

50 Sir Henry Harcourt-Reilly —
[*Stops and stares at* REILLY]

REILLY

[*Without looking up from his papers*]
Good morning, Mr. Chamberlayne.
Please sit down. I won't keep you a moment.
— Now, Mr. Chamberlayne?

106

EDWARD
                    It came into my mind
Before I entered the door, that you might be the same
        person:
But I dismissed that as just another symptom.
Well, I should have known better than to come here
On the recommendation of a man who did not know you.*
Yet Alex is so plausible. And his recommendations
Of shops, have always been satisfactory.
I beg your pardon. But he *is* a blunderer.
I should like to know . . . but what is the use!   60
I suppose I might as well go away at once.

REILLY
No. If you please, sit down, Mr. Chamberlayne.
You are not going away, so you might as well sit down.
You were going to ask a question.

EDWARD
                        When you came to my flat
Had you been invited by my wife as a guest
As I supposed? . . . Or did she *send* you?

REILLY
I cannot say that I had been invited;
And Mrs. Chamberlayne did not know that I was coming.
But I knew you would be there, and whom I should find
        with you.

EDWARD
But you had seen my wife?   70

REILLY
                Oh yes, I had seen her.

107

EDWARD

So this *is* a trap!

REILLY

Let's not call it a trap.
But if it is a trap, then you cannot escape from it:
And so . . . you might as well sit down.
I think you will find that chair comfortable.

EDWARD

You knew,
Before I began to tell you, what had happened?

REILLY

That is so, that is so. But all in good time.
Let us dismiss that question for the moment.
Tell me first, about the difficulties
On which you want my professional opinion.

EDWARD

80 It's not for me to blame you for bringing my wife back,
I suppose. You seemed to be trying to persuade me
That I was better off without her. But didn't you realise
That I was in no state to make a decision?

REILLY

If I had not brought your wife back, Mr. Chamberlayne,
Do you suppose that things would be any better — now?

EDWARD

I don't know, I'm sure. They could hardly be worse.

REILLY

They might be much worse.* You might have ruined three
    lives

108

By your indecision. Now there are only two —
Which you still have the chance of redeeming from ruin.

EDWARD

You talk as if I was capable of action: 90
If I were, I should not need to consult you
Or anyone else. I came here as a patient.
If you take no interest in my case, I can go elsewhere.

REILLY

You have reason to believe that you are very ill?

EDWARD

I should have thought a doctor could see that for himself.
Or at least that he would enquire about the symptoms.
Two people advised me recently,*
Almost in the same words, that I ought to see a doctor.
They said — again, in almost the same words —
That I was on the edge of a nervous breakdown.   100
I didn't know it then myself — but if they saw it
I should have thought that a doctor could see it.

REILLY

'Nervous breakdown' is a term I never use:
It can mean almost anything.

EDWARD

                    And since then, I have realised
That mine is a very unusual case.

REILLY

All cases are unique, and very similar to others.

EDWARD

Is there a sanatorium to which you send such patients

As myself, under your personal observation?

REILLY

You are very impetuous, Mr. Chamberlayne.
110 There are several kinds of sanatoria
For several kinds of patient. And there are also patients
For whom a sanatorium is the worst place possible.
We must first find out what is wrong with you
Before we decide what to do with you.

EDWARD

I doubt if you have ever had a case like mine:
I have ceased to believe in my own personality.

REILLY

Oh, dear yes; this is serious. A very common malady.
Very prevalent indeed.

EDWARD
I remember, in my childhood . . .

REILLY

I always begin from the immediate situation
120 And then go back as far as I find necessary.
You see, your memories of childhood —
I mean, in your present state of mind —
Would be largely fictitious; and as for your dreams,
You would produce amazing dreams, to oblige me.
I could make you dream any kind of dream I suggested,
And it would only go to flatter your vanity
With the temporary stimulus of feeling interesting.

EDWARD

But I am obsessed by the thought of my own insignificance.

REILLY

Precisely. And I could make you feel important,
And you would imagine it a marvellous cure;　　130
And you would go on, doing such amount of mischief
As lay within your power — until you came to grief.
Half of the harm that is done in this world
Is due to people who want to feel important.
They don't mean to do harm — but the harm does not
　　interest them.
Or they do not see it, or they justify it
Because they are absorbed in the endless struggle
To think well of themselves.

EDWARD

　　If I am like that
I must have done a great deal of harm.

REILLY

Oh, not so much as you would like to think:　　140
Only, shall we say, within your modest capacity.
Try to explain what has happened since I left you.

EDWARD

I see now why I wanted my wife to come back.
It was because of what she had made me into.
We had not been alone again for fifteen minutes
Before I felt, and still more acutely —
Indeed, acutely, perhaps, for the first time,
The whole oppression, the unreality
Of the role she had always imposed upon me
With the obstinate, unconscious, sub-human strength　　150

111

That some women have. Without her, it was vacancy.
When I thought she had left me, I began to dissolve,
To cease to exist. That was what she had done to me!
I cannot live with her — that is now intolerable;
I cannot live without her, for she has made me incapable
Of having any existence of my own.
That is what she has done to me in five years together!
She has made the world a place I cannot live in
Except on her terms. I must be alone,
160   But not in the same world. So I want you to put me
Into your sanatorium. I could be alone there?

                    [*House-telephone rings*]

Reilly

[*Into telephone*]   Yes.
[*To* Edward]   Yes, you could be alone there.

Edward

                                    I wonder
If you have understood a word of what I have been saying.

Reilly

You must have patience with me, Mr. Chamberlayne:
I learn a good deal by merely observing you,
And letting you talk as long as you please,
And taking note of what you do not say.

Edward

I once experienced the extreme of physical pain,
And now I know there is suffering worse than that.
It is surprising, if one had time to be surprised:
170   I am not afraid of the death of the body,
But this death is terrifying. The death of the spirit —
Can you understand what I suffer?

REILLY
I understand what you mean.

EDWARD
I can no longer act for myself.
Coming to see you — that's the last decision
I was capable of making. I am in your hands.
I cannot take any further responsibility.

REILLY
Many patients come in that belief.

EDWARD
And now will you send me to the sanatorium?

REILLY
You have nothing else to tell me?*

EDWARD
                        What else can I tell you?
You didn't want to hear about my early history.   180

REILLY
No, I did not want to hear about your *early* history.

EDWARD
And so will you send me to the sanatorium?
I can't go home again. And at my club
They won't let you keep a room for more than seven days;
I haven't the courage to go to a hotel,
And besides, I need more shirts — you can get my wife
To have my things sent on: whatever I shall need.
But of course you mustn't tell her where I am.
Is it far to go?

REILLY

You might say, a long journey.
190 But before I treat a patient like yourself
I need to know a great deal more about him,
Than the patient himself can always tell me.
Indeed, it is often the case that my patients
Are only pieces of a total situation
Which I have to explore. The single patient
Who is ill by himself, is rather the exception.
I have recently had another patient
Whose situation is much the same as your own.
      [*Presses the bell on his desk three times*]
You must accept a rather unusual procedure:
200 I propose to introduce you to the other patient.

EDWARD

What do you mean? Who is this other patient?
I consider this very unprofessional conduct —
I will not discuss my case before another patient.

REILLY

On the contrary. That is the only way
In which it can be discussed. You have told me nothing.
You have had the opportunity, and you have said enough
To convince me that you have been making up your case
So to speak, as you went along. A barrister
Ought to know his brief before he enters the court.

EDWARD

210 I am at least free to leave. And I propose to do so.
My mind is made up. I shall go to a hotel.

REILLY

It is just because you are not free, Mr. Chamberlayne,

114

That you have come to me. It is for me to give you that —
Your freedom. That is my affair.
    [Lavinia *is shown in by the* Nurse-Secretary]
But here is the other patient.

Edward
Lavinia!

Lavinia
                Well, Sir Henry!
I said I would come to talk about my husband:
I didn't say I was prepared to meet him.

Edward
And I did not expect to meet *you*, Lavinia.
I call this a very dishonourable trick.

Reilly
Honesty before honour,* Mr. Chamberlayne.   220
Sit down, please, both of you. Mrs. Chamberlayne,
Your husband wishes to enter a sanatorium,
And that is a question which naturally concerns you.

Edward
I am not going to any sanatorium.
I am going to a hotel. And I shall ask you, Lavinia,
To be so good as to send me on some clothes.

Lavinia
Oh, to what hotel?

Edward
          I don't know — I mean to say,
That doesn't concern you.

LAVINIA
In that case, Edward,
I don't think your clothes concern me either.
[*To* REILLY]
230   I presume you will send him to the same sanatorium
To which you sent me? Well, he needs it more than I did.

REILLY
I am glad that you have come to see it in that light —
At least, for the moment. But, Mrs. Chamberlayne,
You have never visited my sanatorium.*

LAVINIA
What do you mean? I asked to be sent
And you took me there. If that was not a sanatorium
What was it?

REILLY
A kind of hotel. A retreat
For people who imagine that they need a respite
From everyday life. They return refreshed;
240   And if they believe it to be a sanatorium
That is good reason for not sending them to one.
The people who need my sort of sanatorium
Are not easily deceived.

LAVINIA
Are you a devil
Or merely a lunatic practical joker?

EDWARD
I incline to the second explanation
Without the qualification 'lunatic'.
Why should *you* go to a sanatorium?

I have never known anyone in my life
With fewer mental complications than you;
You're stronger than a . . . battleship. That's what drove me   250
     mad.
I am the one who needs a sanatorium —
But I'm not going there.

REILLY
                    You are right, Mr. Chamberlayne.
You are no case for my sanatorium :
You are much too ill.*

EDWARD
                    Much too ill?
Then I'll go and be ill in a suburban boarding-house.

LAVINIA
That would never suit you, Edward. Now I know of a hotel
In the New Forest . . .

EDWARD
                    How like you, Lavinia.
You always know of something better.

LAVINIA
It's only that I have a more practical mind
Than you have, Edward. You do know that.   260

EDWARD
Only because you've told me so often.
I'd like to see *you* filling up an income-tax form.

LAVINIA
Don't be silly, Edward. When I say practical,
I mean practical in the things that really matter.

117

REILLY

May I interrupt this interesting discussion?
I say you are both too ill. There several symptoms
Which must occur together, and to a marked degree,
To qualify a patient for *my* sanatorium:
And one of them is an honest mind.
270   That is one of the causes of their suffering.

LAVINIA

No one can say my husband has an honest mind.

EDWARD

And I could not honestly say that of *you*, Lavinia.

REILLY

I congratulate you both on your perspicacity.
Your sympathetic understanding of each other
Will prepare you to appreciate what I have to say to you.
I do not trouble myself with the common cheat,
Or with the insuperably, innocently dull:
My patients such as you are the self-deceivers
Taking infinite pains, exhausting their energy,
280   Yet never quite successful. You have both of you pretended
To be consulting me; both, tried to impose upon me
Your own diagnosis, and prescribe your own cure.
But when you put yourselves into hands like mine
You surrender a great deal more than you meant to.
This is the consequence of trying to lie to me.

LAVINIA

I did not come here to be insulted.

REILLY

You have come where the word 'insult' has no meaning;*

118

And you must put up with that. All that you have told me —
Both of you — was true enough: you described your
      feelings —
Or some of them — omitting the important facts.   290
Let me take your husband first.
             [*To* EDWARD]
                    You were lying to me
By concealing your relations with Miss Coplestone.

EDWARD
This is monstrous! My wife knew nothing about it.

LAVINIA
Really, Edward! Even if I'd been blind
There were plenty of people to let me know about it.
I wonder if there was anyone who didn't know.

REILLY
There was one, in fact.* But you, Mrs. Chamberlayne,
Tried to make me believe that it was this discovery
Precipitated what you called your nervous breakdown.

LAVINIA
But it's true! I was completely prostrated;   300
Even if I have made a partial recovery.

REILLY
Certainly, you were completely prostrated,
And certainly, you have somewhat recovered.
But you failed to mention that the cause of your distress
Was the defection of your lover — who suddenly
For the first time in his life, fell in love with someone,
And with someone of whom you had reason to be jealous.

EDWARD

Really, Lavinia! This is very interesting.
You seem to have been much more successful at concealment
310 Than I was. Now I wonder who it could have been.

LAVINIA

Well, tell him if you like.

REILLY
                A young man named Peter.

EDWARD

Peter? Peter who?

REILLY
                Mr. Peter Quilpe
Was a frequent guest.

EDWARD
                Peter Quilpe.
Peter Quilpe! Really Lavinia!
I congratulate you. You could not have chosen
Anyone I was less likely to suspect.
And then he came to *me* to confide about Celia!
I have never heard anything so utterly ludicrous:
This is the best joke that ever happened.

LAVINIA

320 I never knew you had such a sense of humour.

REILLY

It is the first more hopeful symptom.

LAVINIA

How did you know all this?

REILLY

     That I cannot disclose.
I have my own method of collecting information
About my patients. You must not ask me to reveal it —
That is a matter of professional etiquette.

LAVINIA

I have not noticed much professional etiquette
About your behaviour to-day.

REILLY

     A point well taken.
But permit me to remark that my revelations
About each of you, to one another,
Have not been of anything that you confided to me.   330
The information I have exchanged between you
Was all obtained from outside sources.
Mrs. Chamberlayne, when you came to me two months ago
I was dissatisfied with your explanation
Of your obvious symptoms of emotional strain
And so I made enquiries.

EDWARD

     It was two months ago
That your breakdown began! And I never noticed it.

LAVINIA

You wouldn't notice anything. You never noticed *me*.

REILLY

Now, I want to point out to both of you
How much you have in common. Indeed, I consider   340
That you are exceptionally well-suited to each other.

Mr. Chamberlayne, when you thought your wife had left
    you,
You discovered, to your surprise and consternation,
That you were not really in love with Miss Coplestone . . .

LAVINIA

My husband has never been in love with anybody.

REILLY

And were not prepared to make the least sacrifice
On her account. This injured your vanity.
You liked to think of yourself as a passionate lover.
Then you realised, what your wife has justly remarked,
350 That you had never been in love with anybody;
Which made you suspect that you were incapable
Of loving. To men of a certain type
The suspicion that they are incapable of loving
Is as disturbing to their self-esteem
As, in cruder men, the fear of impotence.

LAVINIA

You *are* cold-hearted, Edward.

REILLY

                    So you say, Mrs. Chamberlayne.
And now, let us turn to your side of the problem.
When you discovered that your young friend
(Though you knew, in your heart, that he was not in love
    with you,
360 And were always humiliated by the awareness
That you had forced him into this position) —
When, I say, you discovered that your young friend
Had actually fallen in love with Miss Coplestone,
It took you some time, I have no doubt,

Before you would admit it. Though perhaps you knew it
Before he did. You pretended to yourself,
I suspect, and for as long as you could,
That he was aiming at a higher social distinction
Than the honour conferred by being *your* lover.
When you had to face the fact that his feelings towards her   370
Were different from any you had aroused in him —
It was a shock. You had wanted to be loved;
You had come to see that no one had ever loved you.
Then you began to fear that no one *could* love you.

EDWARD
I'm beginning to feel very sorry for you, Lavinia.
You know, you really are exceptionally unlovable,
And I never quite knew why. I thought it was *my* fault.

REILLY
And now you begin to see, I hope,
How much you have in common. The same isolation.
A man who finds himself incapable of loving   380
And a woman who finds that no man can love her.

LAVINIA
It seems to me that what we have in common
Might be just enough to make us loathe one another.*

REILLY
See it rather as the bond which holds you together.
While still in a state of unenlightenment,
You could always say: 'he could not love any woman;'
You could always say: 'no man could love her.'
You could accuse each other of your own faults,
And so could avoid understanding each other.
Now, you have only to reverse the propositions   390
And put them together.

LAVINIA
Is that possible?

REILLY
If I had sent either of you to the sanatorium
In the state in which you came to me — I tell you this:
It would have been a horror beyond your imagining,
For you would have been left with what you brought with
      you:
The shadow of desires of desires.* A prey
To the devils who arrive at their plenitude of power*
When they have you to themselves.

LAVINIA
                              Then what can we do
When we can go neither back nor forward? Edward!*
400   What can we do?

REILLY
                    You have answered your own question,
Though you do not know the meaning of what you have
      said.*

EDWARD
Lavinia, we must make the best of a bad job.
That is what he means.

REILLY
                    When you find, Mr. Chamberlayne,
The best of a bad job is all any of us make of it —
Except of course, the saints — such as those who go
To the sanatorium — you will forget this phrase,
And in forgetting it will alter the condition.

LAVINIA

Edward, there *is* that hotel in the New Forest
If you want to go there. The proprietor
Who has just taken over, is a friend of Alex's.   410
I could go down with you, and then leave you there
If you want to be alone . . .

EDWARD
But I can't go away!
I have a case coming on next Monday.

LAVINIA

Then will you stop at your club?

EDWARD
No, they won't let me.
I must leave tomorrow — but how did you know
I was staying at the club?

LAVINIA
Really, Edward!
I have *some* sense of responsibility.*
I was going to leave some shirts there for you.

EDWARD

It seems to me that I might as well go home.

LAVINIA

Then we can share a taxi, and be economical.   420
Edward, have you anything else to ask him
Before we go?

EDWARD
Yes, I have.
But it's difficult to say.

125

LAVINIA

But I wish you would say it.
At least, there is something I would like you to ask.

EDWARD

It's about the future of . . . the others.
I don't want to build on other people's ruins.

LAVINIA

Exactly. And I have a question too.
Sir Henry, was it you who sent those telegrams?

REILLY

I think I will dispose of your husband's problem.
[*To* EDWARD]
430 Your business is not to clear your conscience
But to learn how to bear the burdens on your conscience.
With the future of the others you are not concerned.

LAVINIA

I think you have answered my question too.*
They had to tell us, themselves, that they had made their
    decision.

EDWARD

Have you anything else to say to us, Sir Henry?

REILLY

No. Not in this capacity.
[EDWARD *takes out his cheque-book.* REILLY *raises his hand.*]
My secretary will send you my account.
Go in peace. And work out your salvation with diligence.*
                                    [*Exeunt* EDWARD *and* LAVINIA]
[REILLY *goes to the couch and lies down. The house-telephone
    rings. He gets up and answers it.*]

126

REILLY

Yes? . . . Yes. Come in.
[*Enter* JULIA by side door]
                    She's waiting downstairs.

JULIA

I know that, Henry. I brought her here myself.   440

REILLY

Oh? You didn't let her know you were seeing me first?

JULIA

Of course not. I dropped her at the door
And went on in the taxi, round the corner;
Waited a moment, and slipped in by the back way.
I only came to tell you, I am sure she is ready
To make a decision.

REILLY

                    Was she reluctant?
Was that why you brought her?

JULIA

                    Oh no, not reluctant:
Only diffident. She cannot believe
That you will take her seriously.

REILLY

                    That is not uncommon.

JULIA

Or that she deserves to be taken seriously.   450

REILLY

That is most uncommon.

JULIA

Henry, get up.
You can't be as tired as that. I shall wait in the next room,
And come back when she's gone.

REILLY

Yes, when she's gone.

JULIA

Will Alex be here?

REILLY

Yes, he'll be here.
[*Exit* JULIA *by side door*]
[REILLY *presses button.*
NURSE-SECRETARY *shows in* CELIA.]

REILLY

Miss Celia Coplestone? . . . Won't you sit down?
I believe you are a friend of Mrs. Shuttlethwaite.

CELIA

Yes, it was Julia . . . Mrs. Shuttlethwaite
Who advised me to come to you. — But I've met you before,
Haven't I, somewhere? . . . Oh, of course.
460   But I didn't know . . .

REILLY

There is nothing you need to know.
I was there at the instance of Mrs. Shuttlethwaite.

CELIA

That makes it even more perplexing. However,
I don't want to waste your time. And I'm awfully afraid
That you'll think that I am wasting it anyway.

128

I suppose most people, when they come to see you,
Are obviously ill, or can give good reasons
For wanting to see you. Well, I can't.
I just came in desperation. And I shan't be offended
If you simply tell me to go away again.

REILLY

Most of my patients begin, Miss Coplestone,   490
By telling me exactly what is the matter with them,
And what I am to do about it. They are quite sure
They have had a nervous breakdown — that is what they
    call it —
And usually they think that someone else is to blame.

CELIA

I at least have no one to blame but myself.

REILLY

And after that, the prologue to my treatment
Is to try to show them that they are mistaken
About the nature of their illness, and lead them to see
That it's not so interesting as they had imagined.
When I get as far as that, there is something to be done.   480

CELIA

Well, I can't pretend that my trouble is interesting;
But I shan't begin that way. I feel perfectly well.
I could lead an active life — if there's anything to work for;
I don't imagine that I am being persecuted;
I don't hear any voices, I have no delusions —
Except that the world I live in seems all a delusion!*
But oughtn't I first to tell you the circumstances?
I'd forgotten that you know nothing about me;
And with what I've been going through, these last weeks,
I somehow took it for granted that I needn't explain myself. 490

E   129

REILLY

I know quite enough about you for the moment:
Try first to describe your present state of mind.

CELIA

Well, there are two things I can't understand,*
Which you might consider symptoms. But first I must tell
    you
That I should really *like* to think there's something wrong
    with me —
Because, if there isn't, then there's something wrong,
Or at least, very different from what it seemed to be,
With the world itself — and that's much more frightening!
That would be terrible. So I'd rather believe
500 There is something wrong with me, that could be put right.
I'd do anything you told me, to get back to normality.

REILLY

We must find out about you, before we decide
What *is* normality.* You say there are two things:
What is the first?

CELIA

An awareness of solitude.
But that sounds so flat. I don't mean simply
That there's been a crash: though indeed there has been.
It isn't simply the end of an illusion
In the ordinary way, or being ditched.
Of course that's something that's always happening
510 To all sorts of people, and they get over it
More or less, or at least they carry on.
No. I mean that what has happened has made me aware
That I've always been alone. That one always is alone.
Not simply the ending of one relationship,

130

Not even simply finding that it never existed —
But a revelation about my relationship
With *everybody*. Do you know —
It no longer seems worth while to *speak* to anyone!*

REILLY

And what about your parents?

CELIA

         Oh, they live in the country,
Now they can't afford to have a place in town.   520
It's all they can do to keep the country house going;
But it's been in the family so long, they won't leave it.

REILLY

And you live in London?

CELIA

         I share a flat
With a cousin: but she's abroad at the moment,
And my family want me to come down and stay with them.
But I just can't face it.

REILLY

So you want to see no one?

CELIA

No . . . it isn't that I *want* to be alone,
But that everyone's alone — or so it seems to me.
They make noises, and think they are talking to each other;
They make faces, and think they understand each other.   530
And I'm sure that they don't. Is that a delusion?

Reilly

A delusion is something we must return from.
There are other states of mind,* which we take to be
    delusion,
But which we have to accept and go on from.
And the second symptom?

Celia

          That's stranger still.
It sounds ridiculous — but the only word for it
That I can find, is a sense of sin.

Reilly

You suffer from a sense of sin, Miss Coplestone?
This is most unusual.

Celia

          It seemed to *me* abnormal.

Reilly

540 We have yet to find what would be normal
For *you*, before we use the term 'abnormal'.
Tell me what you mean by a sense of sin.

Celia

It's much easier to tell you what I don't mean:
I don't mean sin in the ordinary sense.

Reilly

And what, in your opinion, is the ordinary sense?

Celia

Well . . . I suppose it's being immoral* —
And I don't feel as if I was immoral:

132

In fact, aren't the people one thinks of as immoral
Just the people who we say have no moral sense?
I've never noticed that immorality   550
Was accompanied by a sense of sin:
At least, I have never come across it.
I suppose it is wicked to hurt other people.
If you know that you're hurting them. I haven't hurt *her*.
I wasn't taking anything away from her —
Anything she wanted. I may have been a fool:
But I don't mind at all having been a fool.

REILLY

And what is the point of view of your family?

CELIA

Well, my bringing up was pretty conventional —
I had always been taught to disbelieve in sin.   560
Oh, I don't mean that it was ever mentioned!*
But anything wrong, from our point of view,
Was either bad form, or was psychological.
And bad form always led to disaster
Because the people one knew disapproved of it.
I don't worry much about form, myself —
But when everything's bad form, or mental kinks,
You either become bad form, and cease to care,
Or else, if you care, you must be kinky.

REILLY

And so you suppose you have what you call a 'kink'?   570

CELIA

But everything seemed so right, at the time!
I've been thinking about it, over and over;
I can see now, it was all a mistake.

133

But I don't see why mistakes should make one feel sinful!
And yet I can't find any other word for it.
It must be some kind of hallucination;
Yet, at the same time, I'm frightened by the fear
That it is more real than anything I believed in.

REILLY

What is more real than anything you believed in?

CELIA

580   It's not the feeling of anything I've ever *done*,
Which I might get away from, or of anything in me
I could get rid of — but of emptiness, of failure
Towards someone, or something, outside of myself;
And I feel I must . . . *atone* — is that the word?
Can you treat a patient for such a state of mind?

REILLY

What had you believed were your relations with this man?

CELIA

Oh, you'd guessed that, had you? That's clever of you.
No, perhaps I made it obvious. You don't need to know
About him, do you?

REILLY
                 No.

CELIA
Perhaps I'm only typical.

REILLY

590   There are different types. Some are rarer than others.

CELIA

Oh, I thought that I was giving him so much!
And he to me — and the giving and the taking
Seemed so right: not in terms of calculation
Of what was good for the persons we had been
But for the new person, *us*. If I could feel
As I did then, even now it would seem right.
And then I found we were only strangers
And that there had been neither giving nor taking
But that we had merely made use of each other
Each for his purpose. That's horrible. Can we only love   600
Something created by our own imagination?
Are we all in fact unloving and unlovable?
Then one *is* alone, and if one is alone
Then lover and belovèd are equally unreal
And the dreamer is no more real than his dreams.

REILLY

And this man. What does he now seem like, to you?

CELIA

Like a child who has wandered into a forest
Playing with an imaginary playmate
And suddenly discovers he is only a child
Lost in a forest, wanting to go home.   610

REILLY

Compassion may be already a clue
Towards finding your own way out of the forest.

CELIA

But even if I find my way out of the forest
I shall be left with the inconsolable memory
Of the treasure I went into the forest to find

135

And never found, and which was not there
And perhaps is not anywhere? But if not anywhere,
Why do I feel guilty at not having found it?

REILLY

Disillusion can become itself an illusion
620   If we rest in it.

CELIA

I cannot argue.*
It's not that I'm afraid of being hurt again:
Nothing again can either hurt or heal.
I have thought at moments that the ecstasy is real
Although those who experience it may have no reality.
For what happened is remembered like a dream
In which one is exalted by intensity of loving
In the spirit, a vibration of delight
Without desire, for desire is fulfilled
In the delight of loving. A state one does not know
630   When awake. But what, or whom I loved,
Or what in me was loving, I do not know.
And if that is all meaningless, I want to be cured
Of a craving for something I cannot find
And of the shame of never finding it.
Can you cure me?

REILLY

The condition is curable.
But the form of treatment must be your own choice:
I cannot choose for you. If that is what you wish,
I can reconcile you to the human condition,
The condition to which some who have gone as far as you
640   Have succeeded in returning.* They may remember
The vision they have had, but they cease to regret it,

Maintain themselves by the common routine,
Learn to avoid excessive expectation,
Become tolerant of themselves and others,
Giving and taking, in the usual actions
What there is to give and take. They do not repine;
Are contented with the morning that separates
And with the evening that brings together
For casual talk before the fire
Two people who know they do not understand each other,   650
Breeding children whom they do not understand
And who will never understand them.

CELIA

Is that the best life?

REILLY

It is a good life. Though you will not know how good
Till you come to the end. But you will want nothing else,
And the other life will be only like a book
You have read once, and lost. In a world of lunacy,
Violence, stupidity, greed . . . it is a good life.

CELIA

I know I ought to be able to accept that
If I might still have it. Yet it leaves me cold.
Perhaps that's just a part of my illness,   660
But I feel it would be a kind of surrender —
No, not a surrender — more like a betrayal.
You see, I think I really had a vision of something
Though I don't know what it is. I don't want to forget it.
I want to live with it. I could do without everything,
Put up with anything, if I might cherish it.
In fact, I think it would really be dishonest
For me, now, to try to make a life with *any*body!

I couldn't give anyone the kind of love —
670   I wish I could — which belongs to that life.
Oh, I'm afraid this sounds like raving!
Or just cantankerousness . . . still,
If there's no other way . . . then I feel just hopeless.

REILLY

There *is* another way, if you have the courage.
The first I could describe in familiar terms
Because you have seen it, as we all have seen it,
Illustrated, more or less, in lives of those about us.
The second is unknown, and so requires faith —
The kind of faith that issues from despair.*
680   The destination cannot be described;
You will know very little until you get there;
You will journey blind. But the way leads towards possession
Of what you have sought for in the wrong place.

CELIA

That sounds like what I want. But what is my duty?

REILLY

Whichever way you choose will prescribe its own duty.

CELIA

Which way is better?

REILLY

      Neither way is better.
Both ways are necessary. It is also necessary
To make a choice between them.

CELIA

      Then I choose the second.

138

REILLY

It is a terrifying journey.

CELIA

I am not frightened
But glad. I suppose it is a lonely way?   690

REILLY

No lonelier than the other. But those who take the other
Can forget their loneliness. You will not forget yours.
Each way means loneliness — and communion.
Both ways avoid the final desolation
Of solitude in the phantasmal world
Of imagination, shuffling memories and desires.

CELIA

That is the hell I have been in.

REILLY

It isn't hell
Till you become incapable of anything else.
Now — do you feel quite sure?

CELIA

I want your second way.
So what am I to do?   700

REILLY

You will go to the sanatorium.

CELIA

Oh, what an anti-climax! I have known people
Who have been to your sanatorium, and come back again —
I don't mean to say they weren't much better for it —
That's why I came to you. But they returned . . .
Well . . . I mean . . . to everyday life.

139

REILLY

True. But the friends you have in mind
Cannot have been to this sanatorium.*
I am very careful whom I send there:
Those who go do not come back as these did.

CELIA

710 It sounds like a prison. But they can't *all* stay there!
I mean, it would make the place so over-crowded.

REILLY

Not very many go. But I said they did not come back
In the sense in which your friends came back.
I did not say they stayed there.

CELIA
                What becomes of them?

REILLY

They choose, Miss Coplestone. Nothing is forced on them.
Some of them return, in a physical sense;
No one disappears. They lead very active lives
Very often, in the world.

CELIA
                How soon will you send me there?

REILLY

How soon will you be ready?

CELIA
                Tonight, by nine o'clock.

REILLY

720 Go home then, and make your preparations.

Here is the address for you to give your friends;
          [*Writes on a slip of paper*]
You had better let your family know at once.
I will send a car for you at nine o'clock.

CELIA

What do I need to take with me?

REILLY
                    Nothing.
Everything you need will be provided for you,
And you will have no expenses at the sanatorium.

CELIA

I don't in the least know what I am doing
Or why I am doing it. There is nothing else to do:
That is the only reason.

REILLY
        It is the best reason.

CELIA

But I know it is I who have made the decision: 730
I must tell you that. Oh, I almost forgot —
May I ask what your fee is?

REILLY
                I have told my secretary
That there is no fee.

CELIA
        But . . .

141

REILLY
For a case like yours
There is no fee.
                    [*Presses button*]

CELIA
                    You have been very kind.

REILLY
Go in peace, my daughter.
Work out your salvation with diligence.
        [NURSE-SECRETARY *appears at door. Exit* CELIA
        REILLY *dials on house-telephone.*]

REILLY
                [*Into telephone*]
It is finished.* You can come in now.
[*Enter* JULIA *by side door*]
She will go far, that one.

JULIA
                Very far, I think.
You do not need to tell me. I knew from the beginning.

REILLY
740   It's the other ones I am worried about.

JULIA
Nonsense, Henry. *I* shall keep an eye on them.

REILLY
To send them back: what have they to go back to?
To the stale food mouldering in the larder,
The stale thoughts mouldering in their minds.

142

Each unable to disguise his own meanness
From himself, because it is known to the other.
It's not the knowledge of the mutual treachery
But the knowledge that the other understands the motive —
Mirror to mirror, reflecting vanity.
I have taken a great risk.   750

JULIA
                         We must always take risks.
That is our destiny. Since you question the decision
What possible alternative can you imagine?

REILLY
None.

JULIA
        Very well then. We must take the risk.
All we could do was to give them the chance.
And now, when they are stripped naked to their souls
And can choose, whether to put on proper costumes
Or huddle quickly into new disguises,
They have, for the first time, somewhere to start from.
Oh, of course, they might just murder each other!
But I don't think they will do that. We shall see.   760
It's the thought of Celia that weighs upon my mind.

REILLY
Of Celia?

JULIA
        Of Celia.

REILLY
                But when I said just now
That she would go far, you agreed with me.

143

JULIA

Oh yes, she will go far. And we know where she is going.
But what do we know of the terrors of the journey?
You and I don't know the process by which the human is
Transhumanised:* what do we know
Of the kind of suffering they must undergo
On the way of illumination?*

REILLY

           Will she be frightened
770 By the first appearance of projected spirits?*

JULIA

Henry, you simply do not understand innocence.
She will be afraid of nothing; she will not even know
That there is anything there to be afraid of.
She is too humble. She will pass between the scolding hills,
Through the valley of derision,* like a child sent on an errand
In eagerness and patience. Yet she must suffer.

REILLY

When I express confidence in anything
You always raise doubts; when I am apprehensive
Then you see no reason for anything but confidence.

JULIA

780 That's one way in which I am so useful to you.
You ought to be grateful.

REILLY

          And when I say to one like her
'Work out your salvation with diligence', I do not
    understand
What I myself am saying.

JULIA

You must accept your limitations.
— But how much longer will Alex keep us waiting?

REILLY

He should be here by now. I'll speak to Miss Barraway.
[*Takes up house-telephone*]
Miss Barraway, when Mr. Gibbs arrives . . .
Oh, very good.
[*To* JULIA]
He's on his way up.
[*Into telephone*]
You may bring the tray in now, Miss Barraway.
[*Enter* ALEX]

ALEX

Well! Well! and how have we got on?

JULIA

Everything is in order.

ALEX

The Chamberlaynes have chosen?

REILLY

They accept their destiny.

ALEX

And *she* has made the choice?   790

REILLY

She will be fetched this evening.
[NURSE-SECRETARY *enters with a tray, a decanter and three
glasses, and exit.* REILLY *pours drinks.*]
And now we are ready to proceed to the libation.*

145

ALEX

The words for the building of the hearth.
                    [*They raise their glasses*]

REILLY

Let them build the hearth
Under the protection of the stars.

ALEX

Let them place a chair each side of it.

JULIA

May the holy ones watch over the roof,
May the Moon herself influence the bed.
                    [*They drink*]

ALEX

The words for those who go upon a journey.

REILLY

Protector of travellers
800 Bless the road.

ALEX

Watch over her in the desert.
Watch over her in the mountain.
Watch over her in the labyrinth.
Watch over her by the quicksand.

JULIA

Protect her from the Voices
Protect her from the Visions
Protect her in the tumult
Protect her in the silence.
                    [*They drink*]

REILLY

There is one for whom the words cannot be spoken.

ALEX

They can not be spoken yet.   810

JULIA
    You mean Peter Quilpe.

REILLY

He has not yet come to where the words are valid.*

JULIA

Shall we ever speak them?

ALEX
    Others, perhaps, will speak them.

You know, I have connections — even in California.*

CURTAIN

Act Three

The drawing-room of the Chamberlaynes' London flat. Two years later. A late afternoon in July. A CATERER'S MAN *is arranging a buffet table.* LAVINIA *enters from side door.*

CATERER'S MAN
Have you any further orders for us, Madam?

LAVINIA
You could bring in the trolley with the glasses
And leave them ready.

CATERER'S MAN
Very good, Madam.
[*Exit.* LAVINIA *looks about the room critically and moves bowl of flowers.*]
[*Re-enter* CATERER'S MAN *with trolley*]

LAVINIA
There, in that corner. That's the most convenient;
You can get in and out. Is there anything you need
That you can't find in the kitchen?

CATERER'S MAN
Nothing, Madam.
Will there be anything more you require?

LAVINIA

Nothing more, I think, till half past six.

[*Exit* CATERER'S MAN]

[EDWARD *lets himself in at the front door*]

EDWARD

I'm in good time, I think. I hope you've not been worrying.

LAVINIA

Oh no. I did in fact ring up your chambers,   10
And your clerk told me you had already left.
But all I rang up for was to reassure you . . .

EDWARD

[*Smiling*]

That you hadn't run away?

LAVINIA

            Now Edward, that's unfair!
You know that we've given *several* parties
In the last two years. And I've attended *all* of them.
I hope you're not too tired?

EDWARD

            Oh no, a quiet day.
Two consultations with solicitors
On quite straightforward cases. It's you who should be tired.*

LAVINIA

I'm not tired yet. But I know that I'll be glad
When it's all over.   20

EDWARD

            I like the dress you're wearing:
I'm glad you put on that one.

149

LAVINIA
Well, Edward!
Do you know it's the first time you've paid me a compliment
Before a party? And that's when one needs them.

EDWARD
Well, you deserve it. — We asked too many people.

LAVINIA
It's true, a great many more accepted
Than we thought would want to come. But what can you do?
There's usually a lot who don't want to come
But all the same would be bitterly offended
To hear we'd given a party without asking them.

EDWARD
30 Perhaps we ought to have arranged to have two parties
Instead of one.

LAVINIA
That's never satisfactory.
Everyone who's asked to either party
Suspects that the other one was more important.

EDWARD
That's true. You have a very practical mind.

LAVINIA
But you know, I don't think that you need worry:
They won't all come, out of those who accepted.
You know we said, 'we can ask twenty more
Because they will be going to the Gunnings instead'.

EDWARD

I know, that's what we said at the time;
But I'd forgotten what the Gunnings' parties were like.
Their guests will get just enough to make them thirsty;   40
They'll come on to us later, roaring for drink.
Well, let's hope that those who come to us early
Will be going on to the Gunnings afterwards,
To make room for those who come from the Gunnings.

LAVINIA

And if it's very crowded, they can't get at the cocktails,
And the man won't be able to take the tray about,
So they'll go away again. Anyway, at that stage
There's nothing whatever you can do about it:
And everyone likes to be seen at a party
Where everybody else is, to show they've been invited.   50
That's what makes it a success. Is that picture straight?

EDWARD

Yes, it is.

LAVINIA

No, it isn't. Do please straighten it.

EDWARD

Is it straight now?

LAVINIA

Too much to the left.

EDWARD

How's that now?

151

LAVINIA

No, I meant the right.
That will do. I'm too tired to bother.

EDWARD

After they're all gone, we will have some champagne.
Just ourselves. You lie down now, Lavinia.
No one will be coming for at least half an hour;
So just stretch out.

LAVINIA

You must sit beside me,
60 Then I can relax.

EDWARD

This is the best moment
Of the whole party.

LAVINIA

Oh no, Edward.
The best moment is the moment it's over;
And then to remember, it's the end of the season
And no more parties.

EDWARD

And no more committees.

LAVINIA

Can we get away soon?

EDWARD

By the end of next week
I shall be quite free.

152

LAVINIA
And we can be alone.
I love that house being so remote.

EDWARD
That's why we took it. And I'm really thankful
To have that excuse for not seeing people;
And you do need to rest now.   70
[*The doorbell rings*]

LAVINIA
Oh, bother!
Now who would come so early? I simply *can't* get up.

CATERER'S MAN
Mrs. Shuttlethwaite!

LAVINIA
Oh, it's Julia!

[*Enter* JULIA]

JULIA
Well, my dears, and here I am!
I seem *literally* to have caught you napping!
I know I'm much too early; but the fact is, my dears,
That I have to go on to the Gunnings' party —
And you know what *they* offer in the way of food and drink!
And I've had to miss my tea, and I'm simply ravenous
And dying of thirst. What can Parkinson's do for me?
Oh yes, I know this is a Parkinson party;   80
I recognised one of their men at the door —
An old friend of mine, in fact. But I'm forgetting!
I've got a surprise: I've brought Alex with me!
He only got back this morning from somewhere —

153

One of his mysterious expeditions,
And we're going to get him to tell us all about it.
But what's become of him?
[*Enter* ALEX]

EDWARD
Well, Alex!
Where on earth do you turn up from?

ALEX
Where on earth? From the east. From Kinkanja —
90   An island that you won't have heard of
Yet. Got back this morning. I heard about your party
And, as I thought you might be leaving for the country,
I said, I must not miss the opportunity
To see Edward and Lavinia.

LAVINIA
How are you, Alex?

ALEX
I did try to get you on the telephone
After lunch, but my secretary couldn't get through to you.
Never mind, I said — to myself, not to her —
Never mind: the unexpected guest
Is the one to whom they give the warmest welcome.
100   I know them well enough for that.

JULIA
But tell us, Alex.
What were you doing in this strange place —
What's it called?

ALEX
Kinkanja.

154

JULIA

What were you doing
In Kinkanja? Visiting some Sultan?
You were shooting tigers?

ALEX

There are no tigers, Julia,
In Kinkanja. And there are no sultans.
I have been staying with the Governor.
Three of us have been out on a tour of inspection
Of local conditions.

JULIA

What about? Monkey nuts?

ALEX

That was a nearer guess than you think.*
No, not monkey nuts. But it had to do with monkeys —   110
Though whether the monkeys are the core of the problem
Or merely a symptom, I am not so sure.
At least, the monkeys have become the pretext
For general unrest amongst the natives.

EDWARD

But how do the monkeys create unrest?

ALEX

To begin with, the monkeys are very destructive . . .

JULIA

You don't need to tell me that monkeys are destructive.
I shall never forget Mary Mallington's monkey,
The horrid little beast —- stole my ticket to Mentone
And I had to travel in a very slow train   120

And in a *couchette*. She was very angry
When I told her the creature ought to be destroyed.

LAVINIA

But can't they exterminate these monkeys
If they are a pest?

ALEX
Unfortunately,
The majority of the natives are heathen:
They hold these monkeys in peculiar veneration
And do not want them killed. So they blame the
      Government
For the damage that the monkeys do.

EDWARD

That seems unreasonable.

ALEX
It is unreasonable,
130   But characteristic. And that's not the worst of it.
Some of the tribes are Christian converts,
And, naturally, take a different view.
They trap the monkeys. And they eat them.
The young monkeys are extremely palatable:
I've cooked them myself . . .

EDWARD
And did anybody eat them
When you cooked them?

ALEX
Oh yes, indeed.
I invented for the natives several new recipes.

156

But you see, what with eating the monkeys
And what with protecting their crops from the monkeys
The Christian natives prosper exceedingly: 140
And that creates friction between them and the others.
And that's the real problem. I hope I'm not boring you?

EDWARD
No indeed: we are anxious to learn the solution.

ALEX
I'm not sure that there *is* any solution.
But even this does not bring us to the heart of the matter.
There are also foreign agitators,
Stirring up trouble . . .

LAVINIA
Why don't you expel them?

ALEX
They are citizens of a friendly neighbouring state
Which we have just recognised. You see, Lavinia,
There are very deep waters.   150

EDWARD
And the agitators;

How do they agitate?

ALEX
By convincing the heathen
That the slaughter of monkeys has put a curse on them
Which can only be removed by slaughtering the Christians.
They have even been persuading some of the converts —
Who, after all, prefer not to be slaughtered —

To relapse into heathendom. So, instead of eating monkeys
They are eating Christians.

JULIA
Who have eaten monkeys.

ALEX
The native is not, I fear, very logical.

JULIA
I wondered where you were taking us, with your monkeys.
160 I thought I was going to dine out on those monkeys:
But one can't dine out on eating Christians —
Even among pagans!*

ALEX
Not on the *whole* story.

EDWARD
And have any of the English residents been murdered?

ALEX
Yes, but they are not usually eaten.
When these people have done with a European
He is, as a rule, no longer fit to eat.

EDWARD
And what has your commission accomplished?

ALEX
We have just drawn up an interim report.

EDWARD
Will it be made public?

ALEX
It cannot be, at present:
There are too many international complications.   170
Eventually, there may be an official publication.

EDWARD
But when?

ALEX
In a year or two.

EDWARD
And meanwhile?

ALEX
Meanwhile the monkeys multiply.

LAVINIA
And the Christians?

ALEX
Ah, the Christians! Now, I think I ought to tell you
About someone you know — or knew . . .

JULIA
Edward!
Somebody must have walked over my grave:
I'm feeling so chilly. Give me some gin.
Not a cocktail. I'm freezing — in July!

CATERER'S MAN
Mr. Quilpe!

EDWARD

     Now who . . .

[*Enter* PETER]

                Why, it's Peter!

LAVINIA

180   Peter!

PETER

     Hullo, everybody!

LAVINIA

     When did you arrive?

PETER

I flew over from New York last night —
I left Los Angeles three days ago.
I saw Sheila Paisley at lunch to-day
And she told me you were giving a party —
She's coming on later, after the Gunnings —
So I said, I really must crash in:
It's my only chance to see Edward and Lavinia.
I'm only over for a week, you see,
And I'm driving down to the country this evening,
190   So I knew you wouldn't mind my looking in so early.
It does seem ages since I last saw any of you!
And how are you, Alex? And dear old Julia!

LAVINIA

So you've just come from New York.

PETER

                 Yes, from New York.

The Bologolomskys saw me off.

You remember Princess Bologolomsky
In the old days? We dined the other night
At the Saffron Monkey. That's the place to go now.

ALEX

How very odd. *My* monkeys are saffron.

PETER

Your monkeys, Alex? I always said
That Alex knew everybody. But I didn't know   200
That he knew any monkeys.

JULIA

        But give us your news;
Give us your news of the world, Peter.
We lead such a quiet life, here in London.

PETER

You always did enjoy a leg-pull, Julia:
But you all know I'm working for Pan-Am-Eagle?

EDWARD

No. Tell us, what is Pan-Am-Eagle?

PETER

You must have been living a quiet life!
Don't you go to the movies?

LAVINIA
Occasionally.

PETER

        Alex knows.

Did you see my last picture, Alex?

F   161

ALEX

210 I knew about it, but I didn't see it.
There is no cinema in Kinkanja.

PETER

Kinkanja? Where's that? They don't have pictures?
Pan-Am-Eagle must look into this.
Perhaps it would be a good place to make one.
— Alex knows all about Pan-Am-Eagle:
It was he who introduced me to the great Bela.

JULIA

And who is the great Bela?

PETER
                    Why, Bela Szogody —
He's my boss. I thought everyone knew *his* name.

JULIA

Is he your connection in California, Alex?

ALEX

220 Yes, we have sometimes obliged each other.

PETER

Well, it was Bela sent me over
Just for a week. And I have my hands full
I'm going down tonight, to Boltwell.

JULIA

To stay with the Duke?

PETER
                    And do him a good turn.
We're making a film of English life
And we want to use Boltwell.

JULIA

                But I understood that Boltwell
Is in a very decayed condition.

PETER

Exactly. It is. And that's why we're interested.
The most decayed noble mansion in England!
At least, of any that are still inhabited.   230
We've got a team of experts over
To study the decay, so as to reproduce it.
Then we build another Boltwell in California.

JULIA

But what is your position, Peter?
Have you become an expert on decaying houses?

PETER

Oh dear no! I've written the script of this film,
And Bela is very pleased with it.
He thought I should see the original Boltwell;
And besides, he thought that as I'm English
I ought to know the best way to handle a duke.   240
Besides that, we've got the casting director:
He's looking for some typical English faces —
Of course, only for minor parts —
And I'll help him decide what faces are typical.

JULIA

Peter, I've thought of a wonderful idea!
I've always wanted to go to California:
Couldn't you persuade your casting director
To take us all over? We're all very typical.

PETER

No, I'm afraid . . .

163

CATERER'S MAN
Sir Henry Harcourt-Reilly!

JULIA
250 Oh, I forgot! I'd another surprise for you.
[*Enter* REILLY]
I want you to meet Sir Henry Harcourt-Reilly —

EDWARD
We're delighted to see him. But we *have* met before.

JULIA
Then if you know him already, you won't be afraid of him.
You know, I was afraid of him at first:
He looks so forbidding . . .

REILLY
My dear Julia,
You are giving me a very bad introduction —
Supposing that an introduction was necessary.

JULIA
My dear Henry, you are interrupting me.

LAVINIA
If you can interrupt Julia, Sir Henry,
260 You are the perfect guest we've been looking for.

REILLY
I should not dream of trying to interrupt Julia . . .

JULIA
But you're both interrupting!

REILLY
Who is interrupting now?

JULIA
Well, you shouldn't interrupt my interruptions:
That's really worse than interrupting.
Now my head's fairly spinning. I must have a cocktail.

EDWARD
[*To* REILLY]
And will you have a cocktail?

REILLY
Might I have a glass of water?

EDWARD
Anything with it?

REILLY
Nothing, thank you.

LAVINIA
May I introduce Mr. Peter Quilpe?
Sir Henry Harcourt-Reilly. Peter's an old friend
Of my husband and myself. Oh, I forgot —   270
[*Turning to* ALEX]
I rather assumed that you knew each other —
I don't know why I should. Mr. MacColgie Gibbs.

ALEX
Indeed, yes, we have met.

REILLY
On several commissions.

JULIA

We've been having such an interesting conversation.
Peter's just over from California
Where he's something very important in films.
He's making a film of English life
And he's going to find parts for all of us. Think of it!

PETER

But, Julia, I was just about to explain —
280 I'm afraid I can't find parts for anybody
In *this* film — it's not my business;
And that's not the way we do it.

JULIA

But, Peter;
If you're taking Boltwell to California
Why can't you take me?

PETER

We're not taking Boltwell.
We reconstruct a Boltwell.

JULIA

Very well, then:
Why not reconstruct *me*? It's very much cheaper.
Oh, dear, I can see you're determined not to have me:
So good-bye to my hopes of seeing California.

PETER

You know you'd never come if we invited you.
290 But there's someone I wanted to ask about,
Who did really want to get into films,
And I always thought she could make a success of it
If she only got the chance. It's Celia Coplestone.

She always wanted to. And now I could help her.
I've already spoken to Bela about her,
And I want to introduce her to our casting director.
I've got an idea for another film.
Can you tell me where she is? I couldn't find her
In the telephone directory.

JULIA

Not in the directory,
Or in any directory. You can tell them now, Alex.   300

LAVINIA

What does Julia mean?

ALEX

I was about to speak of her
When you came in, Peter. I'm afraid you can't have Celia.

PETER

Oh . . . Is she married?

ALEX

Not married, but dead.*

LAVINIA

Celia?

ALEX

Dead.

PETER

Dead. That knocks the bottom out of it.

EDWARD

Celia dead.

167

JULIA

You had better tell them, Alex,
The news that you bring back from Kinkanja.

LAVINIA

Kinkanja? What was Celia doing in Kinkanja?
We heard that she had joined some nursing order . . .

ALEX

She had joined an order. A very austere one.
310   And as she already had experience of nursing . . .

LAVINIA

Yes, she had been a V.A.D. I remember.*

ALEX

She was directed to Kinkanja,
Where there are various endemic diseases
Besides, of course, those brought by Europeans,
And where the conditions are favourable to plague.

EDWARD

Go on.

ALEX

It seems that there were three of them —
Three sisters at this station, in a Christian village;
And half the natives were dying of pestilence.
They must have been overworked for weeks.

EDWARD

320   And then?

ALEX

And then, the insurrection broke out
Among the heathen, of which I was telling you.

168

They knew of it, but would not leave the dying natives.
Eventually, two of them escaped:
One died in the jungle, and the other
Will never be fit for normal life again.
But Celia Coplestone, she was taken.
When our people got there, they questioned the villagers —
Those who survived. And then they found her body,
Or at least, they found the traces of it.

EDWARD

But before that . . .   330

ALEX
It was difficult to tell.

But from what we know of local practices
It would seem that she must have been crucified
Very near an ant-hill.

LAVINIA
But Celia! . . . Of all people . . .

EDWARD

And just for a handful of plague-stricken natives
Who would have died anyway.

ALEX
Yes, the patients died anyway;

Being tainted with the plague, they were not eaten.

LAVINIA

Oh, Edward, I'm so sorry — what a feeble thing to say!
But you know what I mean.

EDWARD
And you know what I'm thinking.

169

PETER

I don't understand at all.* But then I've been away
340 For two years, and don't know what happened
To Celia, during those two years.
Two years! Thinking about Celia.

EDWARD

It's the waste that I resent.

PETER

You know more than I do:
For *me*, it's everything else that's a waste.
Two years! And it was all a mistake.
Julia! Why don't *you* say anything?

JULIA

You gave her those two years, as best you could.

PETER

When did she . . . take up this career?

JULIA

Two years ago.

PETER

Two years ago! I tried to forget about her,
350 Until I began to think myself a success
And got a little more self-confidence;
And then I thought about her again. More and more.
At first I did not want to know about Celia
And so I never asked. Then I wanted to know
And did not dare to ask. It took all my courage
To ask you about her just now; but I never thought
Of anything like this. I suppose I didn't know her,
I didn't understand her. I understand nothing.

REILLY

You understand your *métier*, Mr. Quilpe —
Which is the most that any of us can ask for.   360

PETER

And what a *métier*! I've tried to believe in it
So that I might believe in myself.
I thought I had ideas to make a revolution
In the cinema, that no one could ignore —
And here I am, making a second-rate film!
But I thought it was going to lead to something better,
And that seemed possible, while Celia was alive.
I wanted it, believed in it, for Celia.
And, of course, I wanted to do something for Celia —
But what mattered was, that Celia was alive.   370
And now it's all worthless. Celia's not alive.

LAVINIA

No, it's not all worthless, Peter. You've only just begun.
I mean, this only brings you to the point
At which you *must* begin. You were saying just now
That you never knew Celia. We none of us did.
What you've been living on is an image of Celia
Which you made for yourself, to meet your own needs.
Peter, please don't think I'm being unkind . . .

PETER

No, I don't think you're being unkind, Lavinia;
And I know that you're right.   380

LAVINIA

                                And perhaps what I've been saying
Will seem less unkind if I can make you understand
That in fact I've been talking about myself.

171

EDWARD

Lavinia is right. This is where you start from.
If you find out now, Peter, things about yourself
That you don't like to face: well, just remember
That some men have to learn much worse things
About themselves, and learn them later
When it's harder to recover, and make a new beginning.
It's not so hard for you. You're naturally good.

PETER

390 I'm sorry. I don't believe I've taken in
All that you've been saying. But I'm grateful all the same.
You know, all the time that you've been talking,
One thought has been going round and round in my head —
That I've only been interested in myself:
And that isn't good enough for Celia.

JULIA

You must have learned how to look at people, Peter,
When you look at them with an eye for the films:
That is, when you're not concerned with yourself
But just being an eye. You will come to think of Celia
400 Like that, one day. And then you'll understand her
And be reconciled, and be happy in the thought of her.

LAVINIA

Sir Henry, there is something I want to say to you.
While Alex was telling us what had happened to Celia
I was looking at your face. And it seemed from your
        expression
That the way in which she died did not disturb you
Or the fact that she died because she would not leave
A few dying natives.

172

REILLY

Who knows, Mrs. Chamberlayne,
The difference that made to the natives who were dying
Or the state of mind in which they died?

LAVINIA

I'm willing to grant that. What struck me, though,   410
Was that your face showed no surprise or horror
At the way in which she died. I don't know if you knew her.
I suspect that you did. In any case you knew *about* her.
Yet I thought your expression was one of . . . satisfaction!

REILLY

Mrs. Chamberlayne, I must be very transparent
Or else you are very perceptive.

JULIA

Oh, Henry!
Lavinia is much more observant than you think.
I believe that she has forced you to a show-down.

REILLY

You state the position correctly, Julia.
Do you mind if I quote poetry, Mrs. Chamberlayne?   420

LAVINIA

Oh no, I should love to hear you speaking poetry . . .

JULIA

She has made a point, Henry.

LAVINIA

. . . if it answers my question.

173

REILLY

Ere Babylon was dust*
The magus Zoroaster, my dead child,
Met his own image walking in the garden.
That apparition, sole of men, he saw.
For know there are two worlds of life and death:
One that which thou beholdest; but the other
Is underneath the grave, where do inhabit
430   *The shadows of all forms that think and live*
Till death unite them and they part no more!

When I first met Miss Coplestone, in this room,
I saw the image, standing behind her chair,
Of a Celia Coplestone whose face showed the astonishment
Of the first five minutes after a violent death.
If this strains your credulity, Mrs. Chamberlayne,
I ask you only to entertain the suggestion
That a sudden intuition, in certain minds,
May tend to express itself at once in a picture.
440   That happens to me, sometimes. So it was obvious
That here was a woman under sentence of death.
That was her destiny. The only question
Then was, what sort of death?* *I* could not know;
Because it was for her to choose the way of life
To lead to death, and, without knowing the end
Yet choose the form of death. We know the death she chose.
I did not know that she would die in this way;
She did not know. So all that I could do
Was to direct her in the way of preparation.
450   That way, which she accepted, led to this death.
And if that is not a happy death, what death is happy?

EDWARD

Do you mean that having chosen this form of death

She did not suffer as ordinary people suffer?

REILLY

Not at all what I mean. Rather the contrary.
I'd say that she suffered all that we should suffer
In fear and pain and loathing — all these together —
And reluctance of the body to become a *thing*.
I'd say she suffered more, because more conscious
Than the rest of us. She paid the highest price
In suffering. That is part of the design.*   460

LAVINIA

Perhaps she had been through greater agony beforehand.
I mean — I know nothing of her last two years.

REILLY

That shows some insight on your part, Mrs. Chamberlayne;
But such experience can only be hinted at
In myths and images.* To speak about it
We talk of darkness, labyrinths, Minotaur terrors.
But that world does not take the place of this one.
Do you imagine that the Saint in the desert
With spiritual evil always at his shoulder
Suffered any less from hunger, damp, exposure,   470
Bowel trouble, and the fear of lions,
Cold of the night and heat of the day, than we should?

EDWARD

But if this was right — if this was right for Celia —
There must be something else that is terribly wrong,*
And the rest of us are somehow involved in the wrong.
I should only speak for myself. I'm sure that *I* am.

REILLY

Let me free your mind from one impediment:

175

You must try to detach yourself from what you still feel
As your responsibility.

EDWARD

           I cannot help the feeling*

480 That, in some way, my responsibility
Is greater than that of a band of half-crazed savages.

LAVINIA

Oh, Edward, I knew! I knew what you were thinking!
Doesn't it help you, that I feel guilty too?

REILLY

If we were all judged according to the consequences
Of all our words and deeds, beyond the intention
And beyond our limited understanding
Of ourselves and others, we should all be condemned.
Mrs. Chamberlayne, I often have to make a decision
Which may mean restoration or ruin to a patient —

490 And sometimes I have made the wrong decision.
As for Miss Coplestone, because you think her death was waste
You blame yourselves, and because you blame yourselves
You think her life was wasted. It was triumphant.
But I am no more responsible for the triumph —
And just as responsible for her death as you are.

LAVINIA

Yet I know I shall go on blaming myself
For being so unkind to her . . . so spiteful.
I shall go on seeing her at the moment
When she said good-bye to us, two years ago.

EDWARD

500 Your responsibility is nothing to mine, Lavinia.

LAVINIA

I'm not sure about that. If I had understood you
Then I might not have misunderstood Celia.

REILLY

You will have to live with these memories and make them
Into something new. Only by acceptance*
Of the past will you alter its meaning.

JULIA

Henry, I think it is time that *I* said something:
Everyone makes a choice, of one kind or another,
And then must take the consequences. Celia chose
A way of which the consequence was Kinkanja.
Peter chose a way that leads him to Boltwell: 510
And he's got to go there . . .

PETER

                    I see what you mean.
I wish I didn't have to. But the car will be waiting,
And the experts — I'd almost forgotten them.
I realise that I can't get out of it —
And what else can I do?

ALEX

                    It is your film.
And I know that Bela expects great things of it.

PETER

So now I'll be going.

EDWARD

                    Shall we see you again, Peter,
Before you leave England?

LAVINIA

Do try to come to see us.
You know, I think it would do us all good —
520 You and me and Edward . . . to talk about Celia

PETER

Thanks very much. But not this time —
I simply shan't be able to.

EDWARD

But on your next visit?

PETER

The next time I come to England, I promise you.
I really do want to see you both, very much.
Good-bye, Julia. Good-bye, Alex. Good-bye, Sir Henry.

[*Exit*]

JULIA

. . . And now the consequences of the Chamberlaynes' choice
Is a cocktail party. They must be ready for it.
Their guests may be arriving at any moment.

REILLY

Julia, you are right. It is also right
530 That the Chamberlaynes should now be giving a party.

LAVINIA

And I have been thinking, for these last five minutes,
How I could face my guests. I wish it was over.
I mean . . . I am glad you came . . . I am glad Alex told us . . .
And Peter had to know . . .

EDWARD

Now I think I understand . . .

178

LAVINIA

Then I hope you will explain it to me!

EDWARD

                Oh, it isn't much
That I understand yet! But Sir Henry has been saying,
I think, that every moment is a fresh beginning;
And Julia, that life is only keeping on;
And somehow, the two ideas seem to fit together.

LAVINIA

But all the same . . . I don't want to see these people.   540

REILLY

It is your appointed burden. And as for the party,
I am sure it will be a success.

JULIA

            And I think, Henry,
That we should leave before the party begins.
They will get on better without us. You too, Alex.

LAVINIA

We don't *want* you to go!

ALEX

          We have another engagement.

REILLY

And on this occasion I shall not be unexpected.

JULIA

Now, Henry. Now, Alex. We're going to the Gunnings.
          [*Exeunt* JULIA, REILLY *and* ALEX]

179

LAVINIA

Edward, how am I looking?

EDWARD
                    Very well.
I might almost say, your best. But you always look your best.

LAVINIA

550 Oh, Edward, that spoils it. No woman can believe
That she always looks her best. You're rather transparent,
You know, when you're trying to cheer me up.
To say I always look my best can only mean the worst.

EDWARD

I never shall learn how to pay a compliment.

LAVINIA

What you should have done was to admire my dress.

EDWARD

But I've already told you how much I like it.

LAVINIA

But so much has happened since then. And besides,
One sometimes likes to hear the same compliment twice.

EDWARD

And now for the party.

LAVINIA
                    Now for the party.

EDWARD

560 It will soon be over.

LAVINIA

I wish it would begin.

EDWARD

There's the doorbell.

LAVINIA

Oh, I'm glad. It's begun.

CURTAIN

Appendix

The tune of *One-Eyed Riley* (page 38), as scored from the author's dictation by Miss Mary Trevelyan.

As I was walk-ing round and round and round in ev'-ry quar-ter I walk'd in to a pub-lic house and or-der'd up my gin and wa-ter

REFRAIN

Too - ri -oo-ley, Too-ri - i-ley, What's the mat-ter with One-Eyed Ri-ley

As I was drink-in' gin and wa-ter (And me be-in' the One-Eyed Ri-ley) Who came in but the land-lord's daugh-ter And she took my heart en-tire-ly

REFRAIN

Too - ri - oo-ley, Too-ri-i-ley, What's the mat-ter with One-Eyed Ri-ley

The Cast of the First Production at the Edinburgh Festival, August 22-27, 1949

Edward Chamberlayne	ROBERT FLEMYNG
Julia (Mrs. Shuttlethwaite)	CATHLEEN NESBITT
Celia Coplestone	IRENE WORTH
Alexander McColgie Gibbs	ERNEST CLARK
Peter Quilpe	DONALD HOUSTON
An Unidentified Guest, *later identified* as Sir Henry Harcourt-Reilly	ALEC GUINNESS
Lavinia Chamberlayne	URSULA JEANS
A Nurse-Secretary	CHRISTINA HORNIMAN
Two Caterer's Men	{ DONALD BAIN MARTIN BECKWITH

Directed by E. MARTIN BROWNE

Settings designed by ANTHONY HOLLAND

Produced by SHEREK PLAYERS LTD.

in association with THE ARTS COUNCIL

2   Some Comments on the Play,
taken from the author's
private correspondence

2 Some Comments on the Play, taken from the author's private correspondence

I would like once again to thank Mrs. Eliot for allowing me the privilege of selecting and publishing the following extracts from her husband's correspondence, for the most part hitherto unpublished, and also for her help and criticism in the work of preparing this edition.

1. From a letter from T. S. Eliot to Mr. Martin Browne, dated 25 January 1948:

> My dear Martin,
>
> I am sorry for the delay in answering your letter of the 19th. I certainly expect the play to be born this year. I do not know how long it will be before it learns to walk, to say nothing of an acrobatic turn worthy of the theatre. Knowing how slowly I work and the amount of time it is likely to take up to get up a head of steam with an engine which has been out of action for so long, I know that the thought of working to a date for this summer would throw me into a panic. I should be quite happy with the prospect of spring 1949, and if, as I hope, I can break the back of the new-born infant during the summer, I should be able to do polishing work even while at Princeton. I hope to be able to start work — or more exactly perhaps I should say sit down morning after morning with nothing else to do — in two or three weeks.

2. The longest and most revealing letter on the play is one written by Eliot in answer to one from his friend and

partner, Sir Geoffrey Faber, whose acutely critical mind touches on many essential points in the play. Extracts from Sir Geoffrey's letter are printed in italics:

(a)   *Aug. 25 '49*
      I do, quite simply, think the play a masterpiece, and as a sexagenarian, I am now qualified to express my admiration — not to say sheer envy — of your power of making new growth. Invention, simplicity of dialogue and versification — these are what make the play so exceptionally impressive. Given, of course, the underlying gravity which is the necessary core of your Ribston Pippin of a Play: but that, as the Daily Graphic *surprisingly perceives, is already known to readers of the* Four Quartets.

(b)   From Eliot's reply, dated 'Trinity XI': 1949 (Postmark = 29 August):

      I am specially gratified by what you say of 'power of making new growth'. This meant a lot to me, because I had always believed a Nobel Prize to be a sort of advance death certificate, and I was putting everything I had into this play in the effort to keep alive.
      (Eliot had been awarded the Nobel Prize in 1948)

(c)   *Heretic as I am — and fear am doomed to remain — in the sense that I am unable to find or to use the prescribed Exit from Hell, I accept your definition of Hell, and on the whole I agree with Reilly's diagnosis. Not entirely by any means . . .*

Sir Geoffrey seems to be referring to the conversation between Reilly and Celia (II. 690–9), where he distinguishes the loneliness felt by the saints (who also have their communion) and the 'solitude in the phantasmal world of imagination, shuffling memories and desires', a kind of lonely Hell within oneself, from which some can find their way out in marriage, in which some communion can be found and the loneliness be forgotten. But even that kind of companionship falls short of perfection, for, as Sir Henry suggests elsewhere (II. 650–2), a kind of contentment is as much as can be hoped for between

> Two people who know they do not understand each other,
> Breeding children whom they do not understand
> And who will never understand them.

This is the passage that Sir Geoffrey Faber considers '*an over-simplification*'. There is another passage in the play that seems relevant to the idea of Hell as loneliness, which appears in an earlier draft as follows:

> *Edward* What is hell? hell is oneself,
>   Hell is alone, the other figures in it
>   One's own projections.

In rewriting the speech in which these lines occur, Eliot salvaged them and they stand virtually unaltered in his final text at I. 3. 417–19. Eliot intended this view of Hell (that Hell is oneself) as a counterblast to the view of Hell (that Hell is other people) presented by Jean-Paul Sartre in *Huis-Clos* (1944), as Martin Browne interestingly records (*The Making of T. S. Eliot's Plays*, p. 233).

Continuing the passage from Sir Geoffrey's letter, at the point at which I interrupted it to explain the references to Hell:

(d)   . . . *The two possible lives, as Reilly states them to Celia, are (I think) a very much too narrow an account of the matter. The lines where Reilly speaks of parents who don't understand each other, and neither understand or are under-*

stood by their children, are not true of marriage and parenthood as I have been fortunate enough to experience these states — far as I fall short of deserving them (and that is not mere conventional modesty). That was the one point in the play where I felt you had perhaps been led by dramatic necessity into an over-simplification which came near to being a falsification. Of course, I know it was Reilly who said it, and not you; and Reilly is not at all to be taken as infallible! All the same . . . there is no correction anywhere else in the play. And perhaps that is because it is concentrated — so far as E. and L. are concerned — upon a marital relationship which doesn't seem even to contain the idea of children.

(e) Eliot's reply, taken from the same letter of 29 August, runs:

About the Choice — ah, yes, of course I must agree, as you put it. But, whatever the point of view, it is obvious that Reilly must make the contrast as sharp as possible; and as for the problem of communication, it is a question of the universe of discourse in which one is moving. There are undoubtedly degrees of understanding — but in the universe of discourse in which Reilly is moving during that speech, there are two primary propositions: (1) nobody understands you but God; (2) all real love is ultimately the love of God.

(f) Oh, and as for Lavinia, I thought it was obvious, from one line at the end of Act III and one line in the opening dialogue of Act IV, that Lavinia was going to have a baby. At her age, I fear it will be an only child . . .

(g) From Mr. Martin Browne, dated 31 March 1949:

. . . I am very glad to hear that the early part of Act IV has gone well in revision. . . . Don't forget Edward and

Lavinia in that latter part: we are very much attached to them by now, and pleased at their achievement of a modus vivendi, so we should like to hear how they managed it — this might well be useful material in the Peter section. I think you will find that in playing they will assume great importance — the play will seem to be largely about them: and on that importance you can build.

It will be seen from the passage I have numbered 2(f) how Eliot responded to this suggestion. I cannot positively identify the 'line at the end of Act III' and the 'line in the opening dialogue of Act IV', because, as will be seen from the next extract, there were changes made in the numbering of the Acts.

3.(a)   Eliot to Mr Martin Browne, 18 July 1948:

Dear Martin,

Having finished the first draft of three acts, I think that I might as well let you have a copy now. The original scheme was for three acts and an 'epilogue'. I have not changed this scheme, but I propose to call the Epilogue 'Act IV'. I think the term 'epilogue', read in the programme, is discouraging for the audience: it suggests that everything will be finished by then, and the epilogue might be omitted.

Act IV, as I now propose it, will repeat the scene, and most of the personages of Act I. The only person absent will of course be Celia. It should be a year, or perhaps two years later than the rest of the play. Some indication of the fate of Celia will be given in the conversation: this is tricky, but I don't want to leave her in the air like Harry. The interesting problem, however, is that of the behaviour of the several persons while Celia is being discussed.

Note: the 'Harry' mentioned here is the protagonist of *The Family Reunion*, who also receives a call to a religious life,

> To the worship in the desert, the thirst and deprivation,
> A stony sanctuary and a primitive altar,
> The heat of the sun and the icy vigil,
> A care over lives of humble people,
> The lesson of ignorance, of incurable diseases.
>
> (*The Family Reunion*, II. 2. 331–5)

We are never told in the play what became of him, in obedience to this call, which nevertheless, like Celia, he obeys, bidding farewell to his family.

(b)   Continuing from Eliot's letter to Mr. Martin Browne of 18 July 1948, we find an early reference to the Libation scene:

> In order to use the same set for Act IV as for Act I, I have put in a final scene at the end of Act III, which was not contemplated in this form when I last saw you, so as to get Julia, Reilly and Gibbs together with all the others out of the way. This is a kind of scene which I, naturally, rather fancy; and which, equally naturally, I fear you will disallow.

(c)   I should think we might allow another 20 pages for the last act. One question will be whether this will work out at anything near the right length. On the one hand, there are probably passages where there are more words than necessary to carry forward the situation, and others where there are gaps. I don't feel that I can myself judge whether I have plotted the emotional curve of the important scenes successfully. One sees the situation at the beginning of the scene, and the situation one wants to arrive at, at the end; but it is, I feel sure, only too easy to leave out indications of sufficient changes, in the course of the dialogue, which the audience must have. I suspect, for instance, that the transformation of Edward and Lavinia, and the development of Celia in the hands of Reilly occurs too abruptly

194

to be convincing. At the same time, I believe that there is always a way of solving the problem *within the time limits of the form*, if one selects the essential words which will do the work within that time. I suppose it is the business of the dramatist to be able to give, in ten minutes on the stage, the illusion of an operation which in life would take at least half an hour.

Yours ever

P.S. I am inclined to think that a better title would be THE COCKTAIL PARTY. A cocktail party of guests whom the host didn't want, corresponds very well to a family reunion from which part of the family was absent.

(It may be noted here that Eliot had at first chosen *One-Eyed Riley* for the title of his comedy, in order strongly to stress the name he had decided to give his principal character; though his identity is not at first disclosed, his raucous music-hall song implants the name which, in its grander form — Sir Henry Harcourt-Reilly — that character will bear. However, as he wrote he changed his mind apparently for the reason here given.)

4.   Eliot to Mr. Martin Browne, dated 15 March 1949:

Dear Martin,

I think it might be possible for me to devise a better opening for Act IV, rewriting the first few pages, and especially if you could allow me a couple of caterer's men to be present at the very beginning. It seems to me that a little business would enliven the opening and stimulate the interest of the audience instead of the mere dialogue. Besides I am not sure that that light comedy dialogue doesn't go on too long and perhaps give the impression of being rather forced.

On the other hand having now worked the thing out to an end I incline to revert to the view that this act works out best timed in this way — *before* the cocktail party — rather than if I tried to reset it to take place just *after* all the other guests had left. I don't mind in the least writing quite a different opening to indicate that the party is over, but if I made that change I wonder whether the conclusion might not be less effective. It seems to me to add to the point of the scene for the audience to have in mind that my people have got to go on with their party in spite of everything; and this ending also seems to provide an effective exit for the other three. I shall be glad if you will think about this carefully. Of course I appear to be assuming that the centre of the scene is all right, and I am certainly not confident about anything.

Yours ever

5. To which Eliot added a postscript on the following day (16 March 1949):

Dear Martin,

A point I forgot. I should like Peter's talk checked to make sure that it does not betray too much ignorance of the film industry. I don't know whether, if he was a script writer, he could be given anything so important to do as engaging minor characters in England. And it is important that his chief interest lay in getting a good part designed for Celia, and persuading her to take it.

Yours ever

6. How willing to change and polish his text, how flexible as a craftsman, how sensitive to the criterion of what will best make its point in a theatre (*'within the time limits of the form'*, to use his own phrase), not only when first putting pen to paper, but also after the play had been successfully performed, may be seen from the following excerpts from two letters to Mr. Martin Browne:

(a)   1st June 1948

Dear Martin,

Here is the first draft of three scenes which I promised you to examine at your convenience. When you are ready for a preliminary talk about it please let me know and we will arrange a meeting.

You will understand of course that this is only a first rough draft and that everything, including a good deal of the actual dialogue, is subject to revision. The verse is still in a very rough state and will in any case need a good deal of polishing. On the other hand I understand how little you can say about what is little more than a third of a play. Possibly no more than whether you think it is worth pursuing or not . . .

The first performance of *The Cocktail Party* was given at the Royal Lyceum Theatre, Edinburgh, as part of the Edinburgh International Festival, on 22 August 1949 and was a nationally acclaimed success. This made a London run during the winter a seeming certainty; but in the event no theatre there was available and the play went to New York instead, where it became the 'talking-point of the season', as Martin Browne records in *The Making of T. S. Eliot's Plays*, p. 241. It opened in London on 3 May 1950 and became, once again, a centre of excited controversy. Eliot was still concerned with perfecting the text, in spite of the praise it had received after the Edinburgh opening, as the following extract from a further letter of his to Martin Browne, dated 7 September 1949 testifies:

(b)   . . . I return from a long week-end in the country, some-what refreshed but still very tired. I am worried by the fact that I have now to prepare three lectures before I go to Germany on October 26th. If the play is to come to London in November, when I shall be away, I shall be hard put to it to effect any actual re-writing . . .

. . . if the play is to be resumed this autumn, or before Christmas, then I must rely upon you pretty heavily for the shortening of it.

I certainly look to Act I (as now constituted) to provide opportunities. I should be sorry to cut the opening, as it seems to me that the light note is very important to the total effect of the play . . .

. . . Well, will you take the initiative about the cutting? I can do a little patchwork in writing in new lines, but I feel quite incapable of thinking the whole play out again for myself.

3   Notes to *The Cocktail Party*

3   Notes to *The Cocktail Party*

ACT I   Scene 1

Lines 14–18

The conversational repetitions in these lines recall the rhythms and repetitions of the first fragment of *Sweeney Agonistes*, which are further marked by thudding rhymes. Here the rhymes have been dropped and the rhythms broken a little, to approximate more closely to normal interchanges of speech, and yet retain the ghost of a feeling of comic verse-energy.

Line 120

Go away yourself! Celia is amazed at the possibility of Edward's vague plan to go away, when the situation as she sees it, specially needs his presence, now that Lavinia has left him and so given him the chance to declare and pursue his relationship with Celia, his mistress; she is confused by his spineless attitude as her next speech shows.

Line 133

Are there any prospects? Julia means will Lavinia's aunt leave her any money? (She is keeping up her pose as a worldly-minded 'tough old woman', as she describes herself in her next speech.)

Line 213

Your wife has left you? The Unidentified Guest asks this question to keep up the pretence of being a stranger to the whole situation, that Edward may converse all the more freely. Actually he knows the whole story as is clear from his confession in Act II, line 70. It is part of the trap in which Edward finds himself at that point.

Line 217

This is an occasion. 'The Unknown Guest warms to his work' Professor John Lawlor, 'The Formal Achievement of *The Cocktail Party*', *Virginia Quarterly Review*, 30, 1954, p. 446.

Line 286

I never thought I should be any happier

With another person. Edward is keeping up the lie he has told in saying that his wife had nothing to complain of in his behaviour (line 231); he is shielding himself and his relationship with Celia.

Lines 328–9

You are nothing but a set

Of obsolete responses. He is a person who has lost the sense of his identity which he had derived from the habits of five years as Lavinia's husband; now that Lavinia has left him, his habits are out of date and he does not know how to respond to events, since the accustomed way has been taken from him. Presently, Edward, unconsciously taking his cue from this speech of the Unidentified Guest, declares '*I must find out who she is, to find out who I am*' (line 356); his Guest is already establishing an authority over him. This is what makes it possible for him to make promises, defy questions and issue orders to Edward, as he does in lines 364, 366 and 374.

Line 384

because one lens is missing. Symbol hunters have linked Julia's one-eyed spectacles with the Unidentified Guest's music-hall ballad of the One-Eyed Riley, and so with the Unidentified Guest himself (Sir Henry Harcourt-Reilly) who in some productions wears a monocle, though this does not appear to be mandatory from the text. D. W. Harding in an essay called 'Progression of Theme in Eliot's Modern Plays' (*Kenyon Review*, Vol. XIII, No. 3, 1956) suggests that

Julia and Sir Henry 'both are metaphorically one-eyed and need each other to give a whole vision'. It is certain that these two need each other; they share the risks they take in pursuing their destiny as Guardians:

Reilly I have taken a great risk.
Julia   We must always take risks.
       That is our destiny.

(II. 750–1)

Moreover their method of working together is later defined by Sir Henry with some clarity:

When I express confidence in anything
You always raise doubts; when I am apprehensive
Then you see no reason for anything but confidence.

(II. 777–9)

But I see no reason to think they are 'metaphorically one-eyed' and need each other to give a whole vision. Spiritual insight is abnormally acute in each of them; there is no point at which Julia's insight corrects Sir Henry's, or his hers. They have different functions of course — she the sheep-dog, he the shepherd — but they have the same visions. The passage about the lost lens can be taken quite simply as a joke — the scatter-brained chatterbox that Julia makes herself out to be in the pretended quest for her spectacles, which are in her pocket all the time, and the joke of a burst of music-hall balladry about the One-Eyed Riley suggested by the one-eyed spectacles and the fact (which we don't yet know) that the Unidentified Guest happens to be called Reilly too.

Line 421

St. Anthony. St. Anthony of Padua (1195–1231), Portuguese by birth, famous preacher in Italy and France, called 'hammer of heretics', and a notable wonder-worker, especially in the matter of finding lost belongings for you. See Donald Attwater, *A Dictionary of Saints* (1958). This is a Christian reference that has slipped out, as it were without Eliot noticing, in Julia's irrepressible rotations of tongue.

Line 507

starting a salon. A way of acquiring social distinction — even fame — by inducing literary lions and lion-cubs to come and prowl round your drawing-room consuming light refreshment and making memorable remarks, on certain regular days; Lavinia's days were Thursdays (line 527); in addition to the lions would be the lionisers, especially women of fashion, such as Celia Coplestone. It is said she was also a poetess, and a good one in line 469; Peter Quilpe was a lion-cub, having published a novel (line 457), and aspiring to direct films. To start a salon, as the word 'salon' suggests (salon = drawing-room) was an idea popular among society hostesses in nineteenth-century Paris.

Line 568

With some secret excitement which I cannot share. Perhaps the excitement of her love for Edward, of which Peter is ignorant. Perhaps an excitement created in her by a more 'indefinable experience' (line 573) than her love for Edward, namely an experience for which her love for Edward turns out to be a substitute, and which ultimately leads to her martyrdom.

Line 601

Excuse me a moment. Edward is being rung by Celia, at an awkward moment. See I. 2. 3.

Line 612

the fool you are. Edward is unconsciously continuing to show how great an influence the Unidentified Guest has already acquired over him, first noted at line 356 (see note to I. 1. 328–9); he is snubbing Peter in much the same way as the Unidentified Guest has snubbed him. He adopts his way

of thinking, when Peter says he must see Celia, by remarking 'Will it be the same Celia?', which recalls the idea of the
Unidentified Guest that our identities change very easily
and swiftly (I. 1. 322–30) and now, in using this phrase to
Peter, he is simply passing on the scornful advice given to
him at line 334, to 'Resign yourself to be the fool you are'.

Line 641

I'd rather you didn't tell her. Peter seems to know that Lavinia
takes a proprietary, almost an amatory interest in him, and
would prefer her not to know of his attachment to Celia, to
avoid a scene with Lavinia.

ACT I   Scene 2

Line 44

Slipper what? One may conjecture that Alex said 'Slivovica',
a Jugoslav brandy made from plums, their national drink;
Edward must have misheard him over the telephone; or
Alex may have got the name a little wrong, since he speaks
of prunes, not plums.

Line 76

He was left at an inn. See Luke 10. 34.

Line 91

He has some sort of power. A spiritual nature like Celia's
might well have unprompted intuitions of this kind; but
perhaps she noticed him at the moment when he had the
strange vision of her he had had standing behind her chair,
which he describes in Act III, lines 425–33, which gave him
the idea that she was 'under sentence of death'.

Line 95

Unless he is the Devil! There is, of course nothing diabolical
about the Unidentified Guest, as some critics have supposed.
He seems diabolical at the moment to Celia because he has

promised to restore Lavinia to Edward's arms, where Celia intends, or thinks she intends to be herself.

Line 150

— *and his name* is *Reilly!* Celia has heard of Sir Henry Harcourt-Reilly from Julia (II. 457–8), but does not yet know he is the Unidentified Guest of Act I scene 1. This is not revealed to her till they meet again in II. 460.

Line 172

I have heard of that experience. Edward, totally immersed in the problems of his own egotism and unable to commit himself or give himself unconditionally to another person, sacrificing all else in his life to it, has never known the kind of ecstasy that his filled Celia, has never been 'in love'. He hotly denies that he has taken Celia '*as a passing diversion*' (I. 2. 191) but the best he seems able to say of her by way of concluding his affair with her is the feeble comment '*And I think you are a very rare person*' (I. 2. 161). We have already heard his advice, or pretended advice, to Peter Quilpe (who believes himself in love with Celia) that it is a mere fever that will cool (I. 1. 579) and that he is to be congratulated on a timely escape (I. 1. 581); this is not the language of a man deeply affected by love or friendship. It may be true that he is trying to protect his relationship with Celia from discovery, and so adopts a cynical tone, but there would be other ways of doing this without such sneers, which either belittle the worth of loving Celia or the worth of his own sincerity towards Peter. He still has much to learn about himself and others.

Line 177

the dream was not enough. Celia hungers for reality thinking to have found it in her love of Edward, which, by the departure of Lavinia, she now feels able to proclaim to the world, and, by a divorce and remarriage, to make real, in the public world, as well as in '*a private world of* ours' (line

170). But now that Edward has repudiated their relationship and says he wishes to have Lavinia back '*the dream was better. It seemed the real reality,*' (I. 2. 179).

Line 181

Perhaps it was I. Unlike most people in such circumstances, Celia blames nobody but herself, and feels humiliated at her own self-betrayal; she makes no reproaches to Edward for letting her down with such a seeming crash; but we are shown at once that this is not due to mere poor-spiritedness in her, but to a real inner magnanimity and sense of truth, for she delivers an annihilating attack on him in her next speech ('Oh, don't think that you can humiliate me!') accusing him of being a self-deceiving sham. This is a true insight into Edward's nature, though during the course of the play, he becomes modestly capable of better things. She does not hit back at him in revenge for having hurt her, but accuses herself of having humiliated herself and her inward vision of love by supposing it could be realised (made real) in Edward. The difference between Edward and Celia can be instantly seen when he feels himself attacked for taking her as a '*passing diversion*' (I. 2. 191); he hits back defensively, but to hurt her, with '*How did you take Peter?*' (line 196). Nevertheless she leads the dialogue back (after this oblique attack has been fended off by her obvious innocence in the matter of Peter) to the central issue, namely that Edward wants Lavinia back, and if that is what suits him, he had better have her back (lines 212–13), and the sooner the better.

Line 220

You should have a man . . . nearer your own age. Perhaps because he is kindled by Celia's intentness on reaching the truth, Edward shows the first signs of a capacity for self-criticism, which increases in strength as the scene progresses. It is as if her sincerity were infectious.

Line 238
But I want to understand you. Here again Celia shows she is
not just striving for victory over Edward in an argument, but
is full of sorrow and compassion for him, for the kind of life
he seems to be choosing; she wants him to be happy, but
how can he be so with Lavinia? (line 243).

Line 244
No — not happy. Edward sunk in the self-absorbed conventional routine of his uninspired character, resigns himself to
it once more, to a meaningless, humdrum existence, after
his recognition of failure to escape into a make-believe love-
affair with Celia. He has met himself as a middle-aged man
(line 229) who feels he has lost the desire for all that was
most desirable, that is (in his idea) for a perfect relationship
in human love and union, having no longer the energy for
it. He sees that he must take what happiness he can from
not having forced himself to continue feeding on an
exhausted passion, which I think may be the sense of his
phrase:

> *of knowing*
> *That the misery does not feed on the ruin of loveliness.*

(I. 2. 246)

Line 247
That the tedium is not the residue of ecstasy. The sense of
ecstasy in a love-relationship is an important criterion to
Eliot. In *The Family Reunion*, Harry says of the relationship between his father and mother 'There was no ecstasy'
(II. 2. 72); for a fuller understanding of the underlying idea,
there could be no better commentary than John Donne's
poem *The Extasie*:

> This Extasie doth unperplex
>   (We said) and tell us what we love,
> Wee see by this, it was not sexe,
>   Wee see, we saw not what did move . . .

> When love, with one another so
>> Interinanimates two soules,
> That abler soule, which thence doth flow,
>> Defects of loneliness controules.

It is a moment of spiritual wonder in a union possible to such as are capable of it; the 'tedium' of which Edward speaks would be the fruit of an attempt to force a continuance of this ineffable experience after it had ceased to 'interinanimate' the lovers.

Line 257

And who in some men may be the guardian. Edward is thinking and talking at a far more perceptive level than one would expect from a man of his conventionality, and there was, in the earlier version of this scene, a passage in which he shows himself aware of this:

> I have had a vision of my own mediocrity;
> But I shall return shortly, I suppose,
> To my proper dimness. Now while I am awake,
> For the first, and for the last time,
> Good-bye.

> (Martin Browne, op. cit., p. 199)

It is to Edward's credit that he has the insight to find the word 'Guardian'. It replaces the word '*daemon*' which is to be found in an earlier draft of the speech we are discussing (lines 244–62). There the lines run:

> I see that my life was determined long ago
> And that the struggle to escape from it
> Is only a make-believe, a pretence
> That what is, is not, or could be changed.
> The self that can say 'I want this — or want that' —
> The self that *wills* — he is a feeble creature;
> He has come to terms in the end
> With the real, tougher self, who does not speak,

Who never talks, who does not argue;
And who in some men may be the daemon, the genius,
And in others, like myself, the dull, implacable,
The indomitable spirit of mediocrity.

(Ibid., pp. 183–4)

Socrates was said to have a *daemon*, or indwelling spirit, to which he gave obedience, a kind of oracle or conscience that seemed to prompt him with a power not his own, not to be disobeyed. It is to some such power Edward is referring, a power that may inspire other men, but not himself; what keeps and prompts Edward is a deadweight of commonplace conventionality. To have realised this is something of an advance in Edward's self-knowledge; perhaps it is Celia's presence that has inspired him to this flight of thought; and a sign of her magnanimity towards him, after he has let her down so unexpectedly, is seen in her willingness to drink a toast with him to 'the Guardians', a word she has done him the honour of borrowing from him. In the earlier version, already quoted from, the toast she proposes is '*To the daemons*' (ibid., p. 200).

Line 267

Twice you have changed. At her first entry in this scene, Edward had appeared to her as the man she loved and was prepared to acknowledge to the world; but his refusal to take the course of claiming his freedom from Lavinia (after her seeming desertion) in order to marry Celia, revealed his mean-hearted, poor-spirited, conventional, mummy-like, dried-up, bloodless nature. That was the first change Celia saw. It was all that was left of what she had thought he was. But now she sees him freshly, as he really is

I see another person,
I see you as a person whom I never saw before.

(I. 2. 283–4)

This is a second change.

Line 285

a projection. That is, an embodiment, in Edward, of a certain vision she had had of the nature of love; it existed in her imagination and she had 'projected' it on him, as one may project a film on a screen; the picture seems to be on the screen, but it 'really' is in the projector.

ACT I   Scene 3

Line 20

To bring someone back from the dead. This is the first fairly explicit reference to the Alcestis theme, from which Eliot tells us the play took its origin. (See Section (h) on Influences and Sources.)

Line 23

Ah, but we die to each other daily. This is a stroke of serious wit by the Unidentified Guest. He is half-quoting from St. Paul's famous phrase in the first Epistle to the Corinthians (Ch. 15. 30–1)

> And why stand we in jeopardy every hour?
> I protest by your rejoicing which I have in Jesus Christ our Lord, I die daily.

St. Paul under constant threat feels his life as a daily death. Sir Henry takes his phrase and plays with it to suggest that human beings are continually ceasing to be what they had seemed to be and becoming something else, as if they had suffered a little death and rebirth. This is illustrated by Celia's remark already noted, that Edward had twice changed while she watched him (I. 2. 267). He had 'died' to her as a lover. The phrase is taken up again later by Lavinia when alone with Edward:

211

I thought that there might be some way out for you
If I went away. *I thought that if I died*
To you, I who had only been a ghost to you,
You might be able to find the road back
To a time when you were real — for you must have
been real
At some time or other, before you ever knew me.

(I. 3. 399–404. My italics)

This willingness to sacrifice herself for Edward reflects the willingness of Alcestis to sacrifice herself for Admetus. The parallel is somewhat faint, but see the note on the word *Dedham* (I. 3. 190).

Line 58

for definite reasons. The Unidentified Guest is allowed to remain unidentified for many reasons; one is Eliot's wish to sustain the mystery and so increase the suspense of the situation for the audience; another reason is that Sir Henry does not wish Edward and Lavinia to realise the trap he has devised for them, from which they could still escape if they knew of it; secondly he wishes them to find themselves bickering just as before, as soon as they are alone together. This will make them both·more than ever convinced that they need his promised help; their waspish incompatibility will also be demonstrated to the audience the first time they are seen left to themselves. For all these reasons, and others, perhaps, Eliot has made Sir Henry keep his secret for a little longer.

Line 72

Julia had a telegram. Here begins the comedy of the telegrams. Julia claims to have had a telegram from Lavinia with a message for Celia. Alex claims to have had a telegram from Lavinia with a message for Peter (line 98). Lavinia knows nothing about the telegrams (line 134) but instantly, and perhaps rightly, judges them to be 'some of

Julia's mischief' (line 138); Alex may have had a hand in it too (line 227). But the simplest explanation is that they were all sent by the Unidentified Guest, with the other Guardians in collusion; the scene makes for lively comedy before the play plunges into the more serious business of the Consulting Room of Sir Henry Harcourt-Reilly.

Line 92

Can't you see me that way too, and laugh about it? Reilly regards the return of a sense of humour as a hopeful symptom (II. 321). Celia has been able to see Edward, first, as the embodiment of the spiritual things she was blindly seeking, then, as a mummy or insect, and, at last, with more truth, as an ordinary human being with absurd foibles and faults, and puffed up with a laughable conceit, blinkered by egotism. To be able to accept all this with a warm laugh is a sign of sanity and friendliness. Celia seems willing to admit she has her own laughable aspects; she says later in Sir Henry's Consulting Room

> I may have been a fool:
> But I don't mind at all having been a fool.
>
> (II. 556)

Line 190

Dedham. Note that this name is rammed into the reader and into the audience — *five times in four lines.* Can it be that the name was chosen by Eliot half as a pun, half as a symbol, to remind us of Alcestis-Lavinia's return from the Home of the Dead (Dead-home)? Of course this would be etymological nonsense, for the name has originally nothing to do with the idea of death, and means 'Dydda's Home' (Eilert Ekwall, *The Concise Oxford Dictionary of English Place-names*, Clarendon Press, 1960); but the sound, so insistently repeated, might recall, to alert eyes and ears, the notion of Lavinia's metaphorical return from the grave.

I can think of no other reason to explain the reiteration; with a writer like Eliot it cannot be an accident.

Lines 220–1

yesterday I started some machine. She started a train of events by leaving Edward which because her action involved the taking of decisions by other people, seems now beyond her control, and indeed is.

Line 224

Somebody is always interfering. She is conscious of the work the Guardians are doing without knowing of their existence.

Line 252

But you *ought to know*. She ought to know because the Unidentified Guest has brought her back, as he promised, and she therefore must know him.

Line 270

And now I can see how absurd you are. Compare Lavinia's manner of announcing this tart discovery with Celia's more affectionate, indulgent way in I. 3. 80–4. So too later in the scene, Lavinia also makes fun of Edward by her school-boy imagery (lines 357–62), but more cuttingly.

Line 327

I was warned of the danger. The danger of returning to the prison-house of matrimonial squabbles with a man who showed no spirit, instead of staying safely in the secluded, restful Hotel-Nursing-Home, which she thinks of as one of Sir Henry's 'sanatoria' (see II. 230–4), and enjoying her 'nervous breakdown'. It must have been Sir Henry who issued the 'warning' she speaks of, using his usual technique with self-obsessed patients like Edward and Lavinia, of advising them to do the opposite of what he intends they shall do, and this drives them into a wilful contradiction of his 'advice' which is just what he has aimed at. In the same way he had seemed to advise Edward that he ought to be thankful for Lavinia's 'desertion',

And yet, the effect of all his argument
Was to make me see that I wanted her back.

(I. 2. 128–9)

Line 357

Oh, Edward, when you were a little boy. See note on line 270 above.

Line 419

Merely projections. See note on I. 2. 285, where Celia's 'projection' was one of love, a heaven of her imagination that she was mistakenly seeing in Edward; here (I. 3. 419) we are told of Edward's projections; locked inside his own self-obsession, he has Hell within him, which he projects upon others, but he is always *alone* in the Hell-prison-cell of Self; contrast Celia, who thinks of this alone-ness of the individual as a 'solitude' of which she has become aware (II. 505), but without fear or regret, and suggests that she is gradually becoming free of worldly attachment (now that Edward has broken her illusion about him) and is approaching a knowledge of the love of God. These two kinds of alone-ness, that at first seem similar, are really opposites. Her whole character and situation reflect the maxim taken by Eliot from St. John of the Cross for the epigraph on *Sweeney Agonistes: 'Hence the soul cannot be possessed of the divine union, until it has divested itself of the love of created beings.'*

Line 423

It was only yesterday. It was only yesterday that Edward had made the decision that he wanted Lavinia back, and that decision has damned him (condemned him) to the old Hell of solitude and total immersion in himself.

Line 451

Celia? Going to California? Yes, with Peter. Lavinia knows perfectly well that this is a false suggestion. She has already been told it is not the case (lines 149–50). Edward cannot have been attending when Peter told Lavinia that he and Celia were not going away together, for now the anguish of having lost Celia strikes him freshly and fiercely, though conventionally too, to make him exclaim:

> O God, O God, if I could return to yesterday
> Before I thought that I had made a decision.
>
> (I. 3. 454–5)

Edward's exclamation had its model in Thomas Heywood's play *A Woman Killed with Kindness* (1603), in Act IV, scene 6:

> O God! O God! that it were possible
> To undo things done; to call back yesterday!

These lines are quoted in Eliot's essay on Thomas Heywood (*Selected Essays*, p. 181), with the comment:

> His nearest approach to those deeper emotions which shake the veil of Time is in that fine speech of Frankford which surely no men or women past their youth can read without a twinge of personal feeling.

The most poignant of all phrases expressing this idea, however, is to be heard in Lady Macbeth's 'What's done cannot be undone.'

ACT II

Line 39

a sanatorium. Sir Henry's connections with sanatoria are never quite clearly defined, nor is it clear what kind of sanatoria they are. We learn from him that '*There are several kinds of sanatoria*' (line 110) for several kinds of patient. Sir Henry evades questions on the subject, but admits in answer to Edward's question whether it was far to go '*You might say, a long journey*' (II. 189). Lavinia believes she has spent some time in one of Sir Henry's sanatoria (II. 230) but he assures her '*You have never visited my sanatorium*' (line 234), as if he only had one after all; he adds that he had sent her to '*a kind if hotel*' (II. 237). People, he says, who need his sanatorium 'are not easily deceived' (line 243) and they must have honest minds (line 269); whereas Edward and Lavinia are self-deceivers (lines 278–80). Those who go to the Sanatorium are the *saints* (line 405). Yet some people have been to Sir Henry's sanatorium, and have come back, 'to everyday life' (II. 705), or so Celia thinks; but Sir Henry mysteriously contradicts her; they cannot have been to the sanatorium, to which he proposes to send Celia (line 707); nevertheless some of those who have been to it have returned 'to lead very active lives, very often, in the world'. (II. 717–18).

To make a guess at the situation behind these hints, Sir Henry has official connections with various kinds of medical, quasi-medical and religious institutions, to which he can send such patients as he judges to be in need of one or other of them; loosely they may all be classed among his 'sanatoria', though they vary from something resembling a private hotel or a nursing-home to the most austere religious, missionary and nursing Orders. This last is a special kind of sanatorium referred to by Sir Henry in II. 234, where those who are not easily deceived are sent (lines 242–3), where also the saints go (line 405). It is to this kind of 'sanatorium' that Celia will be sent; when fully trained there, she will return to lead a very active life in the world, yet no longer in London Society, but among plague-stricken natives in the Christianised parts of Kinkanja, as we learn from Alex in III. 310, and the lines that follow.

Line 56

a man who did not know you. Edward is of course mistaken in thinking Alex does not know Sir Henry; the Guardians keep their association secret to the end.

Line 87

They might be much worse. If he had not decided that he wanted Lavinia back he might have lived with Celia and allowed Lavinia to divorce him. This would have ruined all three of them, in Sir Henry's opinion; and we are meant to agree with him.

Line 97

Two people advised me recently. Celia in Act I scene 2 line 150, and Lavinia in Act I scene 3 line 428.

Line 179

You have nothing else to tell me? Sir Henry is giving Edward a chance to tell the full truth about his situation in regard to Celia as well as to Lavinia, but Edward dodges the question.

Line 220

Honesty before honour, Mr. Chamberlayne. Edward has accused Sir Henry of behaving dishonourably by his breach of confidence in exposing him to his wife, and by disregarding the medical convention by which the secrets of a patient are never divulged to an outsider. Sir Henry raps out this epigram rather slickly; what he means is that Edward has been suppressing the truth about himself and Celia, and this is more important than a fine point in medical etiquette.

Line 234

You have never visited my sanatorium. See note on Act II, line 39.

Line 254

You are much too ill. He is morally ill, self-centred and dishonest; he is in no condition for undertaking the kind of life to which a saint is called; truthfulness and humility such as we shall presently see in Celia are the first requisites, the signs of the spiritual health and strength that she has and he has not. Therefore Sir Henry's special kind of 'sanatorium' is not for him. He presently tells Edward and Lavinia that *you are both too ill* (line 266); and this is apparent from their embittered interchanges.

Line 287

where the word 'insult' has no meaning. In a Consulting Room a truthful diagnosis is what you go for; it is not a personal but a scientific matter to be told the nature of your complaint, whether the knowledge be painful or not.

Line 297

There was one, in fact. Peter Quilpe, of course.

Line 383

just enough to make us loathe one another; another 'point well taken'. Sir Henry is taking a great risk as he very fully understands and later acknowledges; see lines 343–51 in this scene.

Line 396

The shadow of desires of desires. Edward would be haunted by the desire to desire Celia; Lavinia would be haunted by a desire to desire Peter; these would be barren desires for a past now impossible or for an impossible future. These barren desires would be all that they had to think about if they had been sent to sanatoria, whether together or separately. It is not absolutely explicit which of Sir Henry's kinds of sanatoria he has in mind, but (since honesty is the criterion for entry into the kind to which Celia will be sent) one may suppose he is thinking of a sanatorium like 'a kind of hotel' mentioned in II. 237.

Line 397

the devils who arrive at their plentitude of power. This is an allusion to Christ's parable of the unclean spirit that returns to a soul it has quitted and finds it clean and

garnished and empty; and it goes out again to collect seven other spirits more wicked than itself; and the last state of that soul is worse than the first (Matthew 12. 43–5).
Line 399
Edward! In the earlier version of this passage, Lavinia does not use his name, as Mr. Martin Browne points out (op. cit., p. 212), but simply says:

> Then what can we do
> When we can go neither back nor forward?

By adding '*Edward!*' she intensifies her anguish of mind by making a personal appeal for his help, as any affectionate wife might make to a trusted husband in a moment of crisis. It is the first time she has used his Christian name without her habitual cold sneer. It gives hope that their marriage may, after all, succeed.
Line 401
Though you do not know the meaning of what you have said. The meaning of what Lavinia has just said (though in saying it she acted impulsively and did not realise that meaning) is that she and Edward must learn how to make a habit of turning towards each other, rather than against each other, in any personal problem, and to respond as allies, rather than by scoring petty points against each other. The result may not be perfect, for this is an imperfect world, but it will help to '*make the best of a bad job*' as Edward says (line 402). This pessimistic view of normal human relationships, which I suppose Edward utters with a rueful look and a half-laugh at his conventional gibe, seems to be echoed and endorsed more seriously by Sir Henry Harcourt-Reilly, in commenting:

> The best of a bad job is all any of us make of it
> Except, of course, the saints . . .

(lines 404–5)

Sir Henry however means more than Edward in using this phrase. He is making reference to the philosophical and theological view that ours is a 'fallen' world, in which, at some point in Time, things went wrong, and a rebellion, in which the human race joined and to which it became permanently committed, broke out against the will of the Creator. In such a world the only way to do better than 'make the best of a bad job' of the world and its ways, is to 'divest itself of the love of created beings' and seek the love and will of God.

Eliot has also expressed this vision of pervading sin in a fallen world and the effort to escape it in a life of sanctity and expiation, in the person of Harry in *The Family Reunion*; there the theme is more powerfully, more poetically, treated, and at greater length. Sir Geoffrey Faber's letter about *The Cocktail Party* and Eliot's reply, is worth study in this context of the discussion of sacred and profane love (see pages 189–92 and 241).

Line 417

Really, Edward! I have some *sense of responsibility*. Deftly Eliot begins to turn our sympathies towards Lavinia; she reveals some thought for others and some practical ability — she has always boasted herself Edward's superior in practical matters (except in things which in her opinion don't really matter, like Income Tax forms) and now, while Edward's mind is still grappling with his moral problem of not wanting 'to build on other people's ruins', she is already able to think in terms of shirts, taxis and telegrams; after all Edward's hesitations, her mind is made up with a snap.

Line 433

I think you have answered my question too. By evading an answer Sir Henry has virtually admitted that the answer should be 'Yes'.

Line 438

work out your salvation with diligence. The last words of the dying Buddha to his disciples.

'But the Buddha laid stress on the final perseverance of the saints, saying that even the least among the disciples who had entered the first path only, still had his heart fixed on the way to perfection, and constantly strove after the three higher paths. "No doubt," he said, "can be found in the mind of a true disciple." After another pause he said, "Behold, now, brethren, this is my exhortation to you. Decay is inherent in all component things. *Work out, therefore, your emancipation with diligence!*" These were the last words the Buddha spoke. . . .'

> (From the translation in Rhys David's *Buddhist Suttas*, quoted in the *Encyclopaedia Britannica*, 11th Edition, p. 742, under the article on Buddha.)

Line 486

Except that the world I live in seems all a delusion! The world of London, especially of fashionable London, 'Unreal City' as Eliot calls it in *The Waste Land*, l. 60.

Line 493

Well, there are two things I can't understand. For some discussion of these, see the Introduction, p. 267.

Line 503

What is *normality*. What is normal for a saint? The question is insisted on again in lines 541–2.

Line 518

It no longer seems worth while to speak *to anyone!* Yet she is speaking to Sir Henry and establishes a genuine communication with him; this must heighten our opinion of him.

Line 533

There are other states of mind. Sir Henry is speaking from experience, as we learn later (III. 434) when he seemed to see the image of Celia standing behind her chair. This he 'accepted and went on from', to use his own phrase.

Line 546

I suppose it's being immoral. Celia seems to say that she has a moral sense, but does not feel as if she had offended against it; immorality, she thinks, is generally held to be the mark of people who are deficient in moral sense; they feel no guilt, though being 'sinful in the ordinary sense'. It must be admitted her thought in this argument is not quite clear; for by being Edward's mistress she has been 'immoral'; in that case she resembles those whose immorality is not accompanied by a sense of sin. The contrast between them and herself is unclear. Her criterion of wickedness is whether your action hurts someone else, and she claims not to have hurt Lavinia by taking Edward from her (lines 555–556). It would be interesting to know what Lavinia would have retorted.

Line 561

Oh, I don't mean that it was ever mentioned! The question of sin is one of those 'overwhelming questions' which J. Alfred Prufrock, in Eliot's poem, may have wanted to ask, but for the fact that it would have been very bad form to do so in polite society. Misbehaviour, by Celia's account, was regarded (in the circles among which they moved, namely the circles of a West End theatre audience) as either something 'not done', or as something for which one could not be held responsible, a kink in one's nature which one had been born with or which one had acquired in infancy. Celia tells us she is indifferent to the disapproval earned by 'bad form' (567) yet she has not ceased to care about her deviation from conventional morality, so she must be 'kinky' (569–70). But now her deviation seems to her just a mistake (573); but why should one feel '*sinful*' for a *mistake*? Yet she can find no other word for her feelings.

However she does find a word — the word *'emptiness'*, and a failure towards something outside herself (582); it is as if she had belittled herself, not lived to her full stature, had let herself down in relation to this 'something', and that she now *ought to make up for it* — to atone. To *atone* is the word she was looking for, and which she finds presently (line 584).

Line 620

I cannot argue. Celia is making a blind attempt to express the newly felt promptings of the mystical side of her nature; for the moment she has passed beyond the grief and shock of the 'crash' (line 506) and being 'ditched' (508) by Edward, to the realisation that she is alone and aware of guilt, or sin, or failure, because of mistaking the love between her and Edward for the real thing; whereas the treasure she was seeking, the love she is looking for, may be an illusion: lover and beloved, dream and dreamer, all equally unreal (605–6); unless the ecstasy of love is real, though those experiencing it have no reality (624), if that is possible. She attempts to describe this ecstasy as 'an intensity of loving in the spirit, a vibration of delight without desire, for desire is fulfilled in the delight of loving' (626–9). But what or whom it is that she loves she does not know, and is ashamed for not being able to find out (634).

Lines 639–40

The condition to which some who have gone as far as you have succeeded in returning. Celia is asking whether she can be cured of a longing for a visionary love she has not found and cannot find, and which may be an illusion. Reilly offers her a choice of alternatives: the first is the possibility of having a glimpse of some spiritual vocation, and of answering it fully enough to reach Celia's condition, without, after all, pursuing it further; it remains with them as a memory and a regret, but the regret diminishes in time. This may be a reflection of the idea summed up in the words of Jesus 'for many be called but few chosen' (Matthew 20. 16). These who are not 'transhumanised' (line 767) come to accept the 'human condition' that finds its way of love in marriage and a family.

Line 679

The kind of faith that issues from despair. A faith in the truth of her vision, though she may despair of finding it. Perhaps Sir Henry is also warning her of what St. John of the Cross calls 'the dark night of the soul', when your vision fails you and nothing is left you but faith. See *The Ascent of Mount Carmel* by St. John of the Cross, mystical Spanish writer (1549–91).

Line 707

Cannot have been to this sanatorium. See note to II. 39.

Line 737

It is finished. The last words spoken by Jesus from the Cross, according to the *Gospel of St. John* (XIX. 30). Sir Henry certainly knows he is quoting these words from the Gospel and applying them to his own work in bringing Celia to a clear decision and the choice of a 'transhumanised' way of life. He does not, however, know that he is speaking prophetically and that Celia too will be crucified; but these three words should alert an audience to an awareness, however dim, of this significance.

Line 767

Transhumanised. This word may be translated as 'brought to a condition of more than human virtue or power; a nature supernaturally lifted above its natural capacity'. Eliot takes it from Dante's *Paradiso*, I. 70–1:

> Transumanar significar per verba
> non si poria.

> ('Words may not tell of that transhuman change')

Line 769

the way of illumination. A phrase reminiscent of the Buddhist way of life which 'conduces to enlightenment by the noble eight-fold path: right views; right intentions; right actions; right livelihood; right effort; right speech; right mindfulness; right concentration'. (*Encyclopaedia Britannica*, 14th Edn., article on *Buddhism.*)

Line 770

projected spirits. Something has been said of 'projections' in the note on I. 3. 419 and I. 2. 285. It is hard to be quite certain what kind of experience Julia is referring to; there are many possibilities. There is, for instance the long tradition of demonic apparition to Christian Saints, such as St. Anthony of St. Dunstan, to tempt or terrify them, and I think we may best imagine what Julia means by imagining ourselves beset by some nightmare of haunting, or of the sense of some supernatural power of pure evil being present, especially in one's moments of solitude or defencelessness and darkness, or of isolation; some such experience as Coleridge paints in *The Ancient Mariner:*

> Like one, that on a lonesome road
> Doth walk in fear and dread,
> And having once turned round walks on,
> And turns no more his head;
> Because he knows, a frightful fiend
> Doth close behind him tread.

Lines 774–5

She will pass between the scolding hills,

Through the valley of derision. I have been unable to recall or trace the source of these allegorical phrases; they are very unlike the language and way of thinking we associate with Julia's rattling tongue; they sound rather as if they had escaped from John Bunyan; Pofessor Grover Smith suggests it is reminiscent of *The Ascent of Mt. Carmel* (*T. S. Eliot's Poetry and Plays*, University of Chicago Press, 1966, p. 226), but I have not found these exact expressions there.

Line 791

And now we are ready to proceed to the libation. See Section (f), pages 270–4.

Line 811

He has not yet come to where the words are valid. Peter is young; a kind of calf-love and an inner conviction that he will become famous as a revolutionary film-director seem to be his highest experiences in the world of the spirit so far; he is in no urgent psychological danger which would give validity to the kind of prayer which the Guardians feel are needed by Celia and the Chamberlaynes.

Line 813

You know, I have connections — even in California. Another example of the irrepressible comedy by which the Guardians send the play spanking along at its most serious moments; the curtain falls on a solemnity of blessing lightened by a laugh.

ACT III

Line 18

It's you who should be tired. Edward thinks Lavinia may be tired after the work of getting things ready for a party, seeing that she is expecting a baby. (See page 192.)

Line 109

That was a nearer guess than you think. Of course Julia is not guessing, as Alex knows perfectly well, but they are playing their habitual game of concealing their secret association as 'Guardians'. Julia knows the whole Kinkanja story, as later appears (III. 300), and she has brought Alex with her to the Chamberlaynes to tell them. It is she who starts the subject (lines 101–3) and, with her usual verve, elicits enough about Kinkanja to amuse and whet our curiosity; but she doesn't allow the whole story to come out until Peter Quilpe and Sir Henry have arrived to complete Alex's audience. Does she know that Peter is on his way? We are not told so in so many words, but Peter informs us that he has had lunch with Sheila Paisley (line 183) and had told her he intended to 'crash in' on the Chamberlaynes' party; so we may well imagine that Sheila told Julia.

Lines 161–2

But one can't dine out on eating Christians —

Even among pagans! Julia (and Eliot) are here referring to their religion-less London Society audiences, who were pagan without being heathen, like the Greeks and Romans; whereas the Kinkanjans were heathen but not pagan.

Line 303

Not married, but dead. Notice the rhythms, and the repetitions of the word *dead* in these lines:

> *Alex*   Not married, but *dead.*
> *Lavinia* Celia?
> *Alex*   *Dead.*
> *Peter*   *Dead.* That knocks the bottom out of it.
> *Edward* Celia *dead.*

I think it likely that Eliot found these irresistibly impressive cadences in Shakespeare's *Antony and Cleopatra*, Act I, scene 2, lines 151 onwards:

> *Antony*   Fulvia is *dead.*
> *Enobarbus* Sir?
> *Antony*   Fulvia is *dead.*
> *Enobarbus* Fulvia?
> *Antony*   *Dead.*

Line 311

Yes, she had been a V.A.D. I remember. The Voluntary Aid Detachment to which nurses belonged in the 1914–18 War.

Line 339

I don't understand at all. The reactions of Lavinia, Edward and Peter to the news of Celia's crucifixion are of some interest, and Martin Browne's notes on the effect of this scene upon audiences are specially helpful; they are given in his *The Making of T. S. Eliot's Plays*, pp. 229–30, from which I make the following quotation:

  (a) The reaction of the three non-guardians to the story didn't seem violent enough.
  (b) *Peter* in particular worried everybody. Why didn't he rebel actively against the Hollywood he only worked in for Celia's sake? How could he, after helpless protests, just go gaily back there?

Lavinia's reaction, though tame in its expression, is generous both to Edward and to Celia; at least she is no longer thinking only about herself. Edward is thinking of Celia and the waste of Celia's life — for that is how it seems to him, not yet having Sir Henry's viewpoint to guide him. Peter is only thinking of himself, and the waste of two years in Hollywood, spent in thinking about Celia and whether he could find a part for her in a film. One can easily see that he 'has not yet come to where the words are valid' (II. 811). He has hardly begun, and that is what Lavinia tries to tell him (III. 374). But it is too late in the play to attempt a rescue for Peter's character; the audience has heard the fate of Celia, with stupefaction for those who do not know the story, and all that it is now waiting for is Sir Henry Harcourt-Reilly to rise to the occasion: and this he does with sudden impressiveness.

Lines 423–31

Ere Babylon was dust . . . part no more! These lines come from Shelley's lyrical drama *Prometheus Unbound* (published in 1820), among the most splendid masterpieces of the Romantic Movement. They are lines 191–9 of Act I, and are spoken to Prometheus by his mother, Earth. The Act opens in a ravine among the icy rocks of the Indian Caucasus, where Prometheus is chained to a precipice. There the Tyrant Jove has decreed he shall stay for ever in unceasing torment. 'Three thousand years of sleep-unsheltered hours' Prometheus has hung there, defiant, but no longer hating his Supreme Adversary; he has even forgotten the words of the earth-shaking curse he had uttered against Jove, and he now addresses the Mountains, Springs, Air and Whirlwinds, asking them what were the words he had spoken. Their voices reply describing their terrible effect, and the voice of Earth joins with theirs; she had heard the curse which he remembers no longer and would now retract, but not before he has been reminded what the actual words of the curse were. Earth replies that they shall be told him. Then comes the passage quoted by Sir Henry, from Earth's speech. Earth is saying that underneath the grave there is another world, a kind of duplicate of the world we know, where the shadows of all that has ever existed, of all that has ever been thought of or imagined, have their being:

> Dreams and the light imaginings of men,
> And all that faith creates or love desires,
> Terrible, strange, sublime and beauteous shapes.

Prometheus (Earth tells him) could call upon his own shadow to tell him what his words had been; for his 'double' is in that shadowy region too: 'Ask and they must reply' she says. She tells him also that death will unite reality and shadow, and then they will part no more.

Sir Henry quotes this mysterious passage to explain a strange experience of his own that he has hitherto kept to himself, namely that at the original cocktail party with which the play opens, he had seen a vision of Celia, close to Celia herself, her double (as it were) from the region described by Shelley, and that her face 'showed the astonishment of the first five minutes after a violent death' (lines 434–5). He had concluded from this vision, insight, or intuition, that she was about to be united with her shadow and was under sentence of death (line 441). For this reason Sir Henry's face had shown no 'surprise or horror' (line 411) at the news from Kinkanja.

Line 443

what sort of death? He could not know whether it was a natural death or a death by martyrdom, 'because it was for her to choose the way of life to lead to death, and without knowing the end, yet choose the form of death.' She had not then made her choice of death by martyrdom.

Line 460

That is part of the design. See pages 273–80.

Lines 465–6

In myths and images. To speak about it

We talk of darkness, labyrinths, Minotaur terrors. Sir Henry is saying that there are spiritual terrors to face in the spiritual world in which Celia had found her vocation, of which we can only speak in imaginative or poetic terms, but they are not the less real for that. The Minotaur was a mythical monster, half-bull, half-man, that was housed in the labyrinth built by Daedalus in Crete. It was fed on human flesh — seven boys and seven girls, sent every year as tribute from Athens. Sir Henry is saying that the horror of 'spiritual evil always at his shoulder' (line 469) felt by the saints can only be described in terms of nightmare and other monstrous imaginations. The Minotaur image has already

231

been suggested in the litany of the Libation scene, in the line:

> Watch over her in the labyrinth

(II. 803)

Lines 473–4

But if this was right — if this was right for Celia —
There must be something else that is terribly wrong. Edward is unconsciously repeating an idea already expressed by Celia (II. 495–9) when she says she would rather believe there was something wrong with *her* than that there was something so massively wrong in the whole world; she never precisely defines what she is thinking of, but it has to do with her discovery of a sense of sin (II. 535–7) and of emptiness and failure in herself, for which she must *atone* (II. 584). Edward puts the thought differently; if Celia was right in making atonement by her crucifixion, then there *is* something massively wrong with a world that calls for such a sacrifice. The idea behind both these passages is the traditional Christian view, to be found in the Thirty-nine Articles (Articles IX and XV particularly), that man's nature is 'inclined to evil', bent, twisted or fallen from its primal innocence, and is born guilty in a guilty world; this is usually called the doctrine of the Fall, or of Original Sin. Our human wills are corrupt from the start; we can only make atonement by surrendering our wills into the will of God. The call to do so is heard and answered by the saints. The way of redemption from the sins of the world was made open to it by the Incarnation and Crucifixion of Christ, in whose footsteps Celia has found her way of love. A sense of sin, or evil, was the first premonition of her conversion as it was also of Harry's conversion in *The Family Reunion*. Harry also chooses a life of expiation. Considered as the hero of a play, however, he is unhappily dislikeable, violent, inconsiderate, contemptuous and abrupt; there is no feeling

that he has won to grace. But with Celia it is different; she is humble; she is capable of love. *The Cocktail Party* marks a great advance in Eliot's power to express the idea of holiness.

Line 479

I cannot help the feeling. Edward, who had self-deceivingly thought himself in love with Celia and had made her his mistress and, after that, had 'ditched her' (to use her own word in II. 508) feels that his behaviour has contributed to her choice of a way of life which resulted in a terrible death for her. Lavinia tries to help Edward to bear this guilt by sharing it, in that she was unkind and spiteful to her (III. 497); as she was in Act I scene 3, 158–60.

Lines 504–5

Only by acceptance of the past will you alter its meaning. To have that knowledge of yourself that the past reveals gives a new perspective, and so a new meaning and purpose in what lies ahead. 'Every moment is a fresh beginning' says Edward, in a sudden understanding (line 537), to which one may add from Eliot's *East Coker*: 'In my beginning is my end.'

4 An Essay on the Structure and Meaning of the Play

4   An Essay on the Structure and Meaning of the Play

(a) *Two modes of comedy and two of love*

Although in some monumental yet admirable way *Murder in the Cathedral* must be rated as Eliot's greatest dramatic masterpiece, I prefer the spanking *allegro* of *The Cocktail Party*, which takes his problems in holiness out of Church in order to show them to us in our comparatively godless daily lives, where we need not keep straight faces for more than a brief moment. As a play it is the easiest, most cursive and actable, intelligently naturalistic yet poetical comedy he has given us, and the readiest of all his comedies to rouse argument and speculation. It gives an amusingly satirical picture of the fashionable West End world of London between the two wars, and yet is charged with a sense of the mystical destiny of a soul chosen for something greater — the soul of a society girl unforeseeably called upon to lay down her life for others in a far-off, primitive and heathen place, and die unknown, the death of martyrdom. This is the greatness of the play, that it not only convincingly presents a spiritual calling of this kind, but also the antics of our secular, modern world of troubled sexual relationships, in what seems a maladjusted marriage, for the cure of which a brilliant psychoanalysis is amusingly presented. All this is done with great vitality, in a continuous blend of laughter and gravity. No other English comedy has linked these two kinds of spiritual quest — the quest for love in marriage and the quest for the love of God. All I have to say of it is an elaboration of this proposition.

In an undated letter about *The Cocktail Party* to its first director, Mr. Martin Browne, Eliot wrote:

> I am not anxious that people should have the play explained to them before they have seen it.

If he had thought of it, he might have added 'or read it'. By placing this essay after the play, as an appendage, rather than before it, as an introduction, I have sought to fall in with Eliot's wishes and to encourage readers to begin with the play itself.

Best of all is to see it in a theatre, without knowing anything about it in advance, but with an eye and an ear open to all impressions; for that is the experience for which it was designed. Next best is to read it; this will give a ghost of the experience at least (for by being printed, a play dies a little death). After that may come a time for discussion and argument, for this play abounds in combative ideas and, if we judge by the critics, may be taken in different ways. But first things should come first; it is a lucid play (in spite of many twists of surprise and paradox) and can easily be taken at sight; but after it has been so taken, questions begin to arise.

The Cocktail Party has the sparkle and dash of a comedy of manners; a brilliant surface, with underlying depths. More and more seriously the strange, spiritual criss-cross of affections, passions and desires that it pictures unfolds itself as the play proceeds; yet it does so with continuous comedy, almost, indeed, with farce — at the least with hilarious touches. Steadily, however, the story intensifies to reach a moment of great gravity and shock, and this (as it were) brings a silence in heaven.

With this silence comes a richer and happier understanding of love, seen in its two-fold aspects — the human or natural (such as is seen in marriage) and the mystical or divine (such as is seen in Christian sanctity and martyrdom) which reconciles grief with joy and makes disaster seem triumphant. It becomes clearer what Eliot meant when he wrote to Sir Geoffrey Faber that there were two primary propositions in the play: (1) nobody understands you but God; (2) all real love is ultimately the love of God.

These propositions are nowhere explicitly stated in the play, but they undergird it, as they assert the supremacy of love, whether on the mystical or on the natural plane. So, after the grave climax to which I have referred, the story can return to laughter, to another cocktail party, and to a new hope.

Two modes of comedy as well as two of love are merged and blended in this unique play — for I know of no other which combines them all. These modes are the *satiric*, which laughs at folly and affectation out of countenance and punishes vanity with ridicule, and the *romantic*, which is centred in the happy fulfilment of love and has a humane sympathy for all its characters, even in their failings, and is touched throughout with poetry. These are the familiar modes of Congreve and Shakespeare* respectively. Even when we laugh at them we are not to stand aloof from them, but rather realise how we fall under the same condemnation; no concept of 'alienation' should separate the characters in the play from the audience and deny them the empathy they invite. (We may recall Eliot's quotation, at the end of 'The Burial of the Dead' that opens *The Waste Land*, taken from the Preface of Baudelaire's *Les Fleurs du Mal*: 'You! hypocrite lecteur! — mon semblable, — mon frère!', which is a repudiation of the idea that we are in a position to withdraw our charity from those a poet has imagined in order that they may seek it.) Tiresome at moments, ridiculous at others, all the characters are basically likable and intelligent, and even if Peter Quilpe is no great genius, he is companionable enough, and was more so in an earlier draft, as we can see from Martin Browne's *The Making of T. S. Eliot's Plays* (pp. 220–5).

As for Edward and Lavinia, with all their faults and follies, we meet with what seems to be the way in which we are intended to regard them in a passage already quoted from Mr. Martin Browne to Eliot:

> *Don't forget Edward and Lavinia in that latter part: we are very much attached to them by now, and pleased at their achievement of a* modus vivendi, *so we should like to hear how they managed it . . . I think you will find that in playing they will assume great importance — the play will seem to be largely* about *them: and on that importance you can build.*

In *The Cocktail Party*, what is satirical and punitive is funny enough; the pompous Edward and the frigid Lavinia are properly exposed to each other and to us, but they accept their humiliation, they take their medicine, and in the end they are cured. What is satirical and Congrevian, then, is overarched by what is romantic and Shakespearian; consequently the dialogue is a blend of wit and poetry; consequently, too (for it is found, notwithstanding his punitive satire, in Congreve as in Shakespeare), love not ridicule, is the heart's core of the comedy. It ends happily for all.

Yet the shadow of death falls darkly over this happy ending. This too is found in Shakespeare, early and late; early in *Love's Labour's Lost* and late in *The Winter's Tale*. The ridicule in *The Cocktail Party* is light, if sharp, not inflicted as a punishment (as in Ben Jonson) but in the form of therapy; the victims recover from their treatment, and because of it, though they are laughable they are likable, and the more so for the amusement given by them in their moments of absurdity, and for their manner of taking their medicine.

Love, as I have said, is also presented under two traditional modes, and we are meant, at the end, to feel that each has been finely fulfilled; one of them heroically. These modes derive their being from the deepest and most ancient roots of religious thought, coming from far beyond Christianity, yet modified through many Christian centuries, in our parts of the world, into distinctively Christian shapes. One of them is that mode which withdraws from the humdrum world of daily secular life under vows of chastity, poverty and obedience, into monasteries and convents, or in missionary and healing work under a religious discipline. The other is that of a life lived in the normal, natural bustle of the world, and which, if moved by love, takes other vows — the vows of marriage, which it calls a sacrament. In both ways of life, love is seen religiously, as a calling, a vocation, either to the love of God, or to the love that makes a human family.

These two loves were so well recognised as normal alternatives that Chaucer, writing in about 1385, assumed them as a matter of course, trotting them out on the tongue of Pandarus, during a conversation with Troilus about his niece Criseyde who, he thinks, might well be capable of a response to love:

> 'Was nevere man or woman yet bigete
> That was unapt to suffren love's hete,
> Celestial, or elles love of kynde.'
> *(Troilus and Criseyde,* I. 977–9)

'Never', he says 'was man or woman yet begotten who was not liable to suffer the pangs of love, natural or celestial.' It was a platitude, almost a proverb. One of Titian's most famous paintings, entitled *Sacred and Profane Love,* is an allegorical presentation of the same basic idea. In *The Cocktail Party* it lies at the heart of the matter; the love of God awakens in Celia Coplestone and a love for each other awakens in Edward Chamberlayne and his wife Lavinia; each love discovers its right fulfilment, one in the making of a saint, and the other in the remaking of a broken marriage. It is asked in the course of the play which way of love is the better, and the answer given is:

> Neither way is better.
> Both ways are necessary.

(II. 686–7)

This is the fourth and culminating study of Christian sainthood to which Eliot has given dramatic form; he had previously shown a great part of his thought on the subject in *The Rock* (1934), *Murder in the Cathedral* (1935), and *The Family Reunion* (1939).* *The Cocktail Party* was written between May 1948 and August 1949, and grows out of all that he had written on it before.

(b) *One group of characters (Julia, Alex, The Unidentified Guest)*

The characters in *The Cocktail Party* resolve themselves into two groups of which we only gradually become aware, as the painful complexities of the outwardly carefree company of the opening scene unfold themselves. They seem at first as casual a collection of friends as might have been met in any fashionable London flat, in the middle of our century, a little after sundown. They exhibit that somewhat forced yet corporate liveliness that is partly due to a loyal wish to keep the party going, and partly to the power of the abundant cocktails that have been, and are being, served to them. The scene has the cut-glass sparkle of bright epigram and anecdote, rewarded with laughter.

The talk is in the hands of two conspicuous guests when the play opens, whose vivacity singles them out as the self-appointed entertainers of the gathering. These, as the programme will tell us, are Mrs. Julia Shuttlethwaite and Mr. Alexander MacColgie Gibbs. Mrs. Shuttlethwaite is of the kind that would obviously be the life (and death) of any party she attended; Mr. Gibbs aids and abets her.

When the curtain rises — for it is a play written for a 'picture-frame stage' that aims at creating an exact illusion of actuality, in the tradition of drawing-room comedy — Alex and Julia have an audience of two, Celia Coplestone, a young and beautiful society girl, and Peter Quilpe, a rather ordinary young man. A little aloof from these, Edward Chamberlayne, their harassed host, is busy with serving and replenishing drinks, and near him is a strange and striking figure whom nobody seems to know; he wears an eye-glass, says little and drinks gin and water; in marked contrast to the volubility of Alexander and Julia, he is monosyllabic.

These three — Julia, Alexander and the as yet Unidentified Guest — dominate the first scene and although we do not yet know that they are working in collusion with each other and are, secretly, a group of benevolent conspirators, they focus our attention as a kind of Clown-Trio at Edward Chamberlayne's rather sparsely attended cocktail party.

But there is a sense of malaise underlying the party spirit, presently voiced by the delightful but intolerable Julia. She turns on the harassed Edward and probes him for information about Lavinia. Where is Lavinia? Why is she not at her party? This is hideously embarrassing for Edward; Lavinia is Edward's wife, and the horrid truth is that he has no idea where she is, for she has left him, that very afternoon, left him with her cocktail party on his hands. Yet to confess such a thing to this talkative old woman would make him look a fool. To avoid looking like a fool is a powerful motive with Edward, who is soon involved in a number of palpable fibs, having been cornered, 'driven into a toil' as Hamlet would say, by the searching questions put to him by Julia. He has been obliged to invent a sick Aunt for Lavinia to be visiting. Nobody believes in the aunt, but everyone pretends to. Meanwhile it is established that Lavinia is not at home, for reasons undisclosed, and that fact is what starts the action of the play, under the cover of the chit-chat and persiflage, the probings and evasions. When Julia feels herself to have sufficiently bared Edward's secret, she sweeps out, taking with her the main body of the party, like an outgoing tide with its foam, to reveal the rock on which Edward's family craft has split — his wife's disappearance; he finds himself alone with that somewhat grotesque yet impressive stranger, the Unidentified Guest.

We can sometimes find relief in confessing to a stranger what we cannot admit to a friend, and Edward falls into this trap — for trap it is, as we begin later to understand, laid by Julia in collaboration with Alex and the Unidentified Guest himself. When left alone with this unknown person, Edward at once announces to him, not without that faint touch of the self-importance we feel when delivering bad news, that his wife has left him. As he does this, the pattern of relationships begins to shift. Edward has abdicated his position as Host in exchange for that of Client; whereas the Unidentified Guest rises in status from that of an oddity to that of an expert; he at once reveals his acute psychological powers, and before he has finished he is ordering Edward about, in the manner of a psychoanalyst with a patient who needs a dose of humiliation. After telling him that his wife's desertion is all for the best, he delivers the brutal but no doubt necessary advice in a sharp line of (seemingly un-intentional) blank verse:

> Resign yourself to be the fool you are.
>
> (I. 1. 334)

Humbled, almost mesmerised as Edward seems to be by this unexpectedly remarkable stranger, he still has some-thing within himself that refuses to admit that Lavinia's desertion may be all for the best. He finds himself domi-nated by an inexplicable need to get her back, if only to find out who and what he is, and who is she? What can have happened to them during their five years of loveless, childless marriage? He had always taken her for granted and now he cannot even recall exactly what she looks like; he is lost in a painful mystery:

> I am not quite sure that I could describe her
> If I had to ask the police to search for her.
> I'm sure I don't know what she was wearing
> When I saw her last. And yet I want her back.
> And I *must* get her back, to find out what has happened
> During the five years that we've been married.
> I must find out who she is, to find out who I am.
>
> (I. 1. 350–6)

Edward's amazing guest seems to understand this too and undertakes, with absolute confidence, to bring Lavinia back to him within twenty-four hours. Astounded that this stranger should seem to know everything about him and to be able to control the movements of his vanished wife, Edward exclaims:

> Do you mean to say that you know where she is?
>
> (I. 1. 365)

and receives the mysterious, yet still authoritative answer:

245

> That question is not worth the trouble of an answer.
> But if I bring her back it must be on one condition:
> That you promise to ask her no questions
> Of where she has been.

(I. 1. 366–9)

Edward meekly gives his promise, and the Unidentified Guest continues:

> In twenty-four hours
> She will come to you here. You will be here to meet her.

(I. 1. 373–4)

This appointment seems to be the climax of the scene, but it is only the first crest in a range of further climaxes. The inescapable Julia (who has already returned to interrupt them to retrieve her umbrella) now bursts in once more to look for her spectacles (which turn out to be in her pocket all the time). Her reappearance has an astonishing effect upon the Unidentified Guest; he turns instantly into a kind of clown, rising tipsily to his feet, and he sings a stanza of a well-known popular ballad, peculiarly appropriate to himself on account of his eye-glass, and his favourite tipple, and to Julia because of her having so suddenly come in:

> *As I was drinkin' gin and water,*
> *And me bein' the One-Eyed Riley,*
> *Who came in but the landlord's daughter*
> *And she took my heart entirely.*

Then, after a swift and sober aside to Edward 'You will keep our appointment?' to which Edward replies 'I shall keep it', he totters out singing the chorus:

> *Tooryooly toory-iley*
> *What's the matter with One-Eyed Riley?*

He has evidently had too much gin, too little water. Julia seems not to know who he is:

246

Edward who *is* that dreadful man? . . .
. . . Tell me about him. You've been *drinking* together!

(I. 1. 392–6)

But drunk as the Unidentified Guest may seem, he has got his message through to her, namely that he has succeeded in securing Edward's co-operation with him in what the audience knows to be the return of Lavinia. This was what Julia had come back to discover; the tale of her lost spectacles was another of her fibs, and when Edward tells her to look in her bag for them, she finds them.

But Julia has another motive in coming back: she has brought Peter back too. He is the sort of young man whom elderly ladies of her social position like to have about, to catch them taxis (I. 1. 177), but she now decants him on the long-suffering Edward, whose one wish is to be alone. We begin, more and more strongly, to suspect that a kind of strategy is being woven around Edward by these three serio-comic figures, Julia, Alex and the One-Eyed Riley, for presently Alex also returns to look in on Edward, ostensibly to cook some supper for him — Alex takes great pride in his gifts as a chef — but actually to get rid of Peter, who by now has had time for the important talk with Edward which he needed and which Julia had dexterously arranged for him — a talk about Celia.

(c) *A second group of characters (Edward, Peter, Celia, Lavinia)*

It must be confessed that there is a regrettable insipidity about Peter Quilpe, so unceremoniously landed, as it were, by Julia on Edward's lap. Peter is in a kind of quandary; he needs to talk about himself to Edward, as Edward had needed to talk about himself to the Unidentified Guest.

Peter's quandary is not a mature matrimonial one, like Edward's; it is a quandary of calf love; he is wondering whether he has been in love, whether he is still in love, whether he is, or has been loved in return, and if so, what has happened to that return of love? Why does Celia — for it is, of course, she of whom he is speaking — no longer seem to wish for his company that had once seemed agreeable to her, as if she were 'preoccupied with some secret excitement' which he cannot share (I. 1. 566–7). Perhaps Edward, as a disinterested friend, could find out from Celia what has happened to produce this estrangement, this fading-out of Celia from Peter's quasi-amorous life?

Eliot seems unconsciously to have written Peter down; he is commonplace and self-absorbed; nothing he says bears the sharp interest of a creative observation, nothing sparks unexpectedly out of him, he carries no feeling of power or imagination — he is supposed to be a young and rising film-director and he believes himself to be revolutionary in that capacity — but one cannot even imagine him handling a prickly film-star let alone a revolution; during the course of the play, he loses his belief, both in films and in himself, but fades out in the direction of Hollywood with a kindly pat on the back from the One-Eyed Riley, Sir Henry Harcourt-Reilly, as we by then will have learnt to call him.

Yet Peter is in some sort useful, since he helps to communicate to us a certain serenity of character in Celia — her power of contemplation, of absorbed attention — he tells us she went alone to concerts and to picture galleries (I. 1. 540) and that when she allowed him to accompany her:

> And I was so happy when we were together —
> So . . . contented, so . . . at peace: I can't express it;
> I had never imagined such quiet happiness.

(I. 1. 550–2)

She stirred in him no desire for possession, but simply for her company, her presence — 'There was such . . . tranquility' (I. 1. 555).

Peter's visit to Edward corrects and gives depth to the first impressions we had of her in the opening scene. Then we were only aware of her young beauty, her height of fashion, her laughter; now we are won over to her by a sense of enrichment in her, of a nature touched, perhaps, by some mystical inwardness.

All this is in preparation for our first full realisation of her nature and circumstances; these are kept back from us until, in the second scene, we at last see her alone with her lover, Edward Chamberlayne; for Celia is Edward's mistress.

This is the first great surprise of the play; only the most percipient member of an audience could guess the relationship in advance. Yet the hints are there in the text, ready to be conveyed by infinitesimal suggestions in timing and tones of an actor's voice, by glances very reserved and yet indicative, by some abruptness, it may be, in their shaking hands at the end of the party; it is a subtlety for the actors to convey:

Celia	Good-bye, Edward
	Shall I see you soon?
Edward	Perhaps. I don't know.
Celia	Perhaps you don't know? Very well, good-bye.
Edward	Good-bye, Celia.

(I. 1. 181–4)

Later on she rings him up, but we can only guess it is she, for we do not hear her name (I. 1. 600). But we hear it in the last lines of the scene in a climax whose significance is not always instantly perceived; we see its importance in retrospect, a quiet climax, pointer towards the main business of the play, the two ways of love that are to branch out of this relationship.

This climax is handled thus:

Edward *picks up the telephone, and dials a number.*
Edward Is Miss Celia Coplestone in? . . . How long ago? . . .
No, it doesn't matter.

(I. 1. 647–8)

So slight are these indications that we cannot fairly blame Peter Quilpe for his maladroit choice of Edward as his confidant. But Peter is too self-absorbed to be aware of what is going on in Edward, that dull grown-up, as he must seem to him, kind but dull; elderly. Yet there is another use in Peter's choice of Edward, a satirical use; for we hear Edward echoing the Unidentified Guest in the advice he gives to Peter; he tells him he is lucky to have escaped from Celia, as he had himself been told he was lucky to have escaped from Lavinia; it was all for the best. And he tells him, rather contemptuously, that he doesn't know why he is taking so much trouble to protect him from the fool he is (I. 1. 611). The influence of the Unidentified Guest is palpable enough: he had used almost the same words to Edward a few moments before (I. 1. 334).

As the curtain falls at the end of Scene 1, Edward, disappointed in his attempt to ring Celia, sits down to play a game of Patience. He is still playing when the curtain rises again; the door-bell rings and he rises to answer. It is Celia. We soon feel her clear and fearless strength. Having given herself wholly to Edward, she is ready, now that Lavinia has left him, for the world to know it; ready to live with him openly through the scandal and difficulties of divorce, ready to take the social blame herself, rather than force him to go through the miserable pretences of adultery; she rejoices at their being at last free to face the world of London society, in which she is so admired a figure, and challenge it with the integrity of her love for Edward. This love, no doubt, was the 'secret excitement' which Peter had said was preoccupying her and which he could not share (I. 1. 561–2).

But Edward has changed. Unaccountably he wants Lavinia back. At first Celia cannot believe it, and puts it down to a temporary weakness, overwork, mental illness; she tries to lend him her strength:

> Will you assure me that everything is right,
> That you do not mean to have Lavinia back
> And that you do mean to gain your freedom,
> And that everything is all right between us?
> That's all that matters. Truly, Edward,
> If that is right, everything else will be,
> I promise you.

> (I. 2. 153–9)

But Edward remains firm in his weakness. It is too late. He is too old. He has lost the desire for all that is most desirable (I. 2. 231–2). There is a kind of climax in self-realisation for each of them as the scene draws to its strange close. Edward sees that the effort to escape from his own mediocrity through his love-affair with Celia, was only a make-believe, a furtive attempt to find a way out of the joyless realities of his marriage:

> a pretence
> That what is, is not, or could be changed.

> (I. 2. 250)

His life had been determined long ago in the conventional ways of the world; his mere emotional wants were not strong enough to compete with the massive, protective inertia of his own commonplaceness. The pretence, he says, could no longer be kept up; and for once Edward, in elaborating this assertion, makes a striking remark, unexpected in so uninspired a man. He says he must submit to the dull, dominating apathy of his nature, which keeps him safe, guards him from adventure, and rules him as much as some other men are ruled by an inner genius:

> . . . the obstinate, the tougher self; who does not speak,
> Who never talks, who cannot argue;
> And who in some men may be the *guardian* —
> But in men like me, the dull, the implacable,
> The indomitable spirit of mediocrity.

(I. 2. 255–9)

As he makes this confession, it seems to Celia that she is witnessing a total change in Edward's nature; it is as if scales had dropped from her eyes and she was seeing him as he really was, and not (as she had imagined him before) a lover matching her in love; this new vision of him she clothes in a poetry of candour well-suited to her, though (since imagery can exaggerate) a little hard on him; she sees him as a mummy being unwrapped, whose voice was the voice of an insect:

> Dry, endless, meaningless, inhuman —

(I. 2. 274)

and whose true likeness appeared to her as 'only a beetle the size of a man', as if he had undergone some hideous metamorphosis, like the unhappy wretch in Kafka's story, *The Metamorphosis*, changed during the night into a beetle:

> With nothing more inside it than what comes out
> When you tread on a beetle

(I. 2. 279–80)

Edward rises to a little moment of greatness by accepting this wounding description as the truth:

> Perhaps that is what I am.
> Tread on me, if you like.

(I. 2. 281–2)

But Celia spares him; she does not reproach him for what he cannot help being, still less does she tread on him; for she now realises her own mistaking. It had been her fault to idealise him, to think he embodied a reality that existed elsewhere, that she was desparately seeking. There is something in her thought that resembles a thought of Madame Odintsov in Turgenev's *Fathers and Sons*:*

> Why is it that when one is enjoying, say, a piece of music or a beautiful summer evening, or a conversation with a sympathetic companion, the occasion seems rather a hint at an infinite felicity existent elsewhere, than a real felicity actually being experienced?

Celia puts it this way, as she meditates her feelings for Edward:

> The man I saw before, he was only a projection —
> I see that now — of something that I wanted —
> No, not *wanted* — something I aspired to —
> Something that I desperately wanted to exist.
> It must happen somewhere — but what, and where is it?
>
> (I. 2. 285–9)

Though she does not yet realise it, it had been a vision of divine love, which she had 'projected' on Edward and of which she only knows, or desparately wishes, that 'it must happen somewhere'. She had thought to find it in a human relationship, but she had been deluded, self-deluded, as she now sees; she must look elsewhere. The last thing she takes from her former lover is his striking phrase, the Guardian; together they drink, at her suggestion, 'to the Guardians.' By the kind of swift, decisive intuition we have come to expect of her, and shall meet in her again, she has seen her need for guidance, and is willing to recognise a Guardian, even in Julia:

> It may be that even Julia is a guardian.
> Perhaps she is *my* guardian.
>
> (I. 2. 311–12)

and this is the truth.

The last member of the second group of characters to appear and be recognised is Lavinia. True to his word the Unidentified Guest produces her in Edward's flat within twenty-four hours. She walks in, unannounced, using her own key, as if she had never been away, as cool as if she were the mistress of the situation. It is the last scene of Act I, the first purpose of which is a long farewell; it is the last that the other characters will see of Peter for a long time; he is off to California. It is the last, though they do not know it, that they will ever see of Celia Coplestone.

But the scene has another purpose; when Celia has gone, followed, after a moment by Julia, Alex and Peter, we are left with Edward and Lavinia, alone together once again, coldly man and wife.

'I must say, you don't seem very pleased to see me', she cannot help remarking (I. 3. 233). Their incompatible cat-and-dog lives recommence. Lavinia cannot resist humiliating her husband; Edward shields himself behind his seemingly invulnerable conventionality. She can now see (she tells him) how absurd he is; he has no sense of humour; he can never make a practical decision. And so the dialogue of polite fury begins again; every repartee hits a tender spot. Yet there are signs of love under the ice:

> O, Edward, I should like to be good to you —
> Or if that's impossible, at least be horrid to you —
> Anything but nothing, which is all you seem to want of me.
>
> (I. 3. 392–4)

and again, when she says:

> I thought that there might be some way out for you
> If I went away. I thought that if I died

> To you, I who had been only a ghost to you,
> You might be able to find the road back
> To a time when you were real —
>
> (I. 3. 399–403)

Edward is no match for her; he is cowed by the knowledge that he might have been free of her, if only he had not insisted on having her brought back to him! She is the angel of destruction. Desperately he is driven to rhetorical questions:

> O God, what have I done? The python. The octopus.
> Must I become after all what you would make me?
>
> (I. 3. 460–1)

She remains the cool mistress of the situation:

> Meanwhile my luggage is in the hall downstairs:
> Will you get the porter to fetch it up for me?
>
> (I. 3. 467–8)

(d) *Guardians and guardianship*

By the end of Act I the exposition is complete. The two groups of characters and their spiritual relationships have been indicated, and all is poised to go forward. Eliot's love of mystification, his talent for creating suspense out of almost nothing, still teases us in the matter of the Unidentified Guest, and though the existence of Guardians has been half-laughingly suggested by Celia, we have as yet no certainty of it. The certainty, however, is not long delayed after we are shown the Consulting Room of Sir Henry Harcourt-Reilly, and recognise him as the One-Eyed Riley of the first Act. That Alexander MacColgie Gibbs and Julia Shuttlethwaite are his secret-service agents is soon obvious enough. They do not think of themselves, never speak of themselves, as Guardians; they give their association no name, but they work together, like a harmonious committee in which each from time to time may take the Chair, though Sir Henry is felt to be their leader, since he has overriding authority as a psychotherapist. This, however, does not prevent Julia from saying what she thinks, with a 'Nonsense, Henry!' when she feels inclined.

Though their association is never revealed by them, or discovered by the others, and the word Guardians is never specifically applied to them in the play, we may take it and use it for the convenience of discussing the work of Sir Henry and his associates, which starts many hares. The first is the symbolic overtone we cannot but hear in the word *Guardian*; it inevitably suggests *Guardian Angel*, and consequently a kind of hint that the Guardians have some supernatural element or authority, a mysterious touch of priesthood, or even of something indefinably more than human, though appearing to be human flesh and blood; or, if that is too extreme a suggestion, they are corporately to be considered as *symbolising* the Church in its care of souls. From this thought it is easy to go further and see in Sir Henry's Consulting Room something analogous to a Confessional, and in the 'Libation scene' (to be discussed later), something suggestive of a sacrament, if not (for Celia, at least) a last sacament, a *viaticum*.

Another significant overtone may be heard from a non-Christian context, the thought of which cannot but have been present to Eliot when he settled on the word *Guardian* to put in Edward's mouth — a context unknown, doubtless to Edward, but very familiar to Eliot, namely that of *The Republic* of Plato. Here, in Plato's blueprint for a perfect State, is a long account of the education proper to its 'Guardians', or philosopher-kings, and their place in the establishment of justice, the essential both for the State and for every individual within it.

Too much weight should not be given to these overtones
or correspondences; it is true that symbolism had always
appealed to Eliot, and this permits the slightly luminous
haze into which such interpretations tempt us to wander
and wonder, without being absolutely misled; but the play
makes very good sense without them, and there are other
aspects of the Guardians that are more fruitful to think
about.

The Family Reunion opens with a situation in the life of a
family cursed with loveless marriage in two consecutive
generations, and we learn, as the play unfolds, a great deal
about its earlier history, which Eliot had imagined and
conveyed in careful detail. But *The Cocktail Party* has no
such long pre-history; at most we can say that if it began
with the marriage of Edward and Lavinia, it began five
years before the opening scene, for Edward tells us so (I. 1.
225). But how or when the Guardians began to form themselves into an active, secret group, we are not told. Clearly,
however, they are by no means beginners. Any account of
them must start with *One-Eyed Riley*, and that was the
title originally proposed by Eliot for the comedy.* This
striking figure with his tipsy snatch of music-hall song is
revealed at the opening of the second Act as Sir Henry
Harcourt-Reilly, a leading psychoanalyst, who pursues
methods of his own in the conduct of his profession, often of
a somewhat unorthodox kind; they include prescribing rest-
cures in secluded '*sanatoria*' that resemble private hotels
rather than clinics, and to these he sends wealthy patients
who are, or believe themselves to be, suffering from 'a
nervous breakdown' — a phrase Sir Henry never uses. But
he is also in touch with certain religious, medical and
missionary Orders, whose religious houses he also calls
'*sanatoria*', and to these he entrusts those patients whose
malaise is a sense of the sins of the world and a spiritual

I   257

craving to expiate or atone for them by a life of dedication, a self-surrender to a power whose beauty and attraction they have felt or glimpsed and which may be called the will or love of God. To enter such a 'sanatorium' is to abandon all earthly ties, other than those to which their Order directs them, such as the care of the sick and destitute, and the extension of their message of love in far countries and among heathen peoples.

Sir Henry's methods of recruiting his patients are also startling, for they include the services of his two socialite assistants (Julia and Alex), who have a gift for sensing where spiritual crises are building up in the circles of their acquaintance. Julia seems to have the keener nose in this respect, and has discerned that all is not well between Edward and Lavinia. She has persuaded Lavinia to become Sir Henry's patient, without her husband's knowledge, a little time before the play begins (II. 230–1). We do not know the nature of Lavinia's malady, but it may be imagined as the effect of five years of a barren and meaningless marriage on a quick-witted and sensitive woman.

Sir Henry decides to send her to one of his secular sanatoria (of the luxury-hotel kind) whither she departs, completely forgetting, if we may believe her assurance (I. 3. 245), that she had invited friends round for cocktails that very afternoon. Sir Henry, however, had not forgotten, and so he arrives as 'an Unidentified Guest', assumed, no doubt, by Edward, Celia and Peter to be a friend of the absent Lavinia. He has thus put himself in a position to observe the immediate effect on Edward of Lavinia's disappearance — (into Sir Henry's 'sanatorium'). His allies, Julia and Alex, take on the task of diverting the company while he observes it. That he is also, and most deeply, observing Celia we learn much later in the play, when he

tells of the strange vision he had had of her at the opening
cocktail party (III. 434–8). Julia had perhaps suggested he
should observe Celia as well as Edward, for Celia too had
been advised by Julia to consult Sir Henry (II. 457). Celia,
like Lavinia, accepts the advice, after the breakdown of her
relationship with Edward. Peter Quilpe, on the periphery
of these crises, is doubly, if dimly, involved; for he imagines
himself to be in love with Celia, while Lavinia imagines
herself to be in love with him (II. 308–15). But the
Guardians realise that Peter is in no need of them; he is not
faced by a momentous spiritual choice, as the others are:
'He has not yet come to where the words are valid', as Sir
Henry puts it, when considering whether the Guardians
should speak a prayer for him (II. 811). For the present all
Peter need do is to pursue his job as a film-director to
the best of his ability; he has no need of either kind of
sanatorium.

But Edward, Celia and Lavinia are in deeper waters, and
Act I pilots them into port, that is, into the Consulting
Room of Sir Henry Harcourt-Reilly, that their hearts may
be laid bare to him, and to us.

Before we watch them enter the sanctum of the One-
Eyed Riley, there is a question to be faced which presses
more and more upon us as we realise how Edward, Celia,
Lavinia and possibly Peter, have been netted by this secret
conspiracy of self-appointed moral straighteners. We feel it
an unwarrantable presumption for the Guardians to inter-
fere, unasked, in the spiritual destinies of three, perhaps
four, souls, who have been manoeuvred into seeking Sir
Henry's advice. This charge against the Guardians is never
levelled in the play, but it is one which audiences are likely
to formulate and hold against them. The charge has some
justice in it, and must be faced later; but first their function
in the play may be considered on a lighter level.

The Guardians are a two-way force or impetus that drives the play along on each of its different planes; the first plane is one of frivolous comedy, rising to farce. They give the play all its comic energy. The play opens with a burst of their laughter and their clowning continues in scene after scene, right up to that moment of supreme gravity and shock when Alex tells us that Celia has been crucified by monkey-worshipping savages near an ant-hill.

In contrary motion, on another plane, not divulged to us until the second Act, the Guardians reveal themselves as people who have secretly, but religiously, banded themselves together, to keep watch over their friends and others whom they know to be reaching a spiritual crisis in their lives. Their business is to shepherd them into the Consulting-Room of their leader, in whose humane wisdom they have put their trust.

As this underlying seriousness unfolds itself and we learn the complexities of the situation, their comic power harnesses itself to their graver purposes, their jokes sparkle through the crises, and there are more music-hall tricks — the greater the gravity, the finer the fun. The tale of Lady Klootz and her false teeth (which never gets told), the tipsy ballad of the One-Eyed Riley, Julia's maddening intrusions in search, first of her umbrella, next of her spectacles, Alex's kindly but infuriating return when he is not wanted, and his insisting on cooking Edward 'a toothsome meal' which uses all tomorrow's breakfast eggs and is burnt to a cinder, the continual ringing of telephone and doorbell, the comedy of the mysterious telegrams — all these things springing from Eliot's comic invention and given to the Guardians, supply the comic energy of the play. It maintains its momentum 'to move wild laughter in the throat of death' right up to the account of the saffron monkeys of Kinkanja, though these preposterous creatures are an indirect cause of Celia's martyrdom; and so we reach the sublime by the ridiculous.

Structurally considered, then, the Guardians correspond in one sense to the Eumenides in *The Family Reunion*; they supply what Dryden or Byron and the older kind of criticism, based on the epic and drama of ancient Greece, might have called 'the supernatural machinery' for they lead in the direction of a supernatural love to which it was Eliot's main hope to awaken his audiences. Yet, as I have claimed, they are not to be thought of as supernatural themselves, but as two men and a woman seeking to do good by stealth through a conspiracy of enlightened benevolence. It is a dangerous trade to play Providence, as the case of the hapless Friar Laurence in *Romeo and Juliet* shows; yet we are moved to accept and delight in the Guardians, as we do in Friar Laurence, though for not the same reasons. We like and forgive them their interference first because they make us laugh; they are the *primum mobile* of the play, the laughter that moves it; secondly they acknowledge that they are working and moving among mysteries beyond their understanding, at least in the case of Celia; even in the cases of Edward and Lavinia Sir Henry admits doubtingly and humbly, that he has 'taken a great risk' (II. 351); as for Celia, he admits:

> And when I say to one like her
> 'Work out your salvation with diligence', I do not understand
> What I myself am saying.
>
> (II. 781–3)

So these seemingly over-reaching clowns, that have taken so much upon themselves, are 'holy and humble men of heart' and earn our affection and respect as healers, as richly as they do as jesters.

It is in embodying the notion of the Guardians, however,

that this play diverges from what it pretends to be — a slice of life cut from the cake-stand of drawing-room comedy; for through the Guardians it enters the world of serious moral questioning. It does so to put forward an answer to one of those 'overwhelming questions' that are not much asked in drawing-rooms; Eliot had remarked on this some seven-and-thirty years before in that brief masterpiece *The Love Song of J. Alfred Prufrock*. Prufrock, the diffident lover, dare not approach the drawing-room of his beloved and formulate any of the disturbing questions that perhaps can only be answered by a Lazarus, that is, by one returned from the dead; for such questions in a drawing-room would seem superfluous, impertinent, irrelevant, unsophisticated. Here, in the Chamberlayne drawing-room, however, the Prufrock in Eliot has plucked up courage, and poses Cain's momentous question:

Am I my brother's keeper?

and to this, the answer given by the play, and by Christianity, is '*Yes, you are.*'

St. Paul said we are all members one of another (*Ephesians* 4. 25). And we may say that if Julia is Celia's Guardian — as Celia thought she might be — then, by a like reasoning, Celia is also Julia's Guardian; it is always the duty of each to care for all and all to care for each, a counsel of perfection, like other unattainable Christian imperatives, and one well known by Eliot. But to ask him to make this larger assertion his theme would be to ask for a different play, or perhaps for any essay; and indeed Eliot *had* written such an essay ten years before, in a series of lectures entitled *The Idea of a Christian Society* (1939).* Mr. David E. Jones and Mr. Martin Browne concur in thinking these lectures are significant in a discussion of the nature of the Guardians; how relevant they are may be seen from the following passages which I have taken from the third lecture; they describe a society in which groups like the Guardians might well exist and operate:

> It would be a society in which the natural end of man — virtue and well-being in community — is acknowledged for all, and the supernatural end — beatitude — for those who have the eye to see it.

> We need therefore what I have called 'The Community of Christians', by which I mean not local groups, and not the Church in any one of its senses, unless we call it 'the Church within the Church'. These will be the consciously and thoughtfully practising Christians, especially those of intellectual and spiritual superiority.

> The Community of Christians is not an organisation, but a body of indefinite outline; composed both of clergy and of laity, of the more conscious, more spiritually developed of both.

and again, in an Appendix, the Church is said to:

> maintain the paradox that while we are responsible for our own souls, we are all responsible for all other souls.

There is something chilling in these concepts; if the Guardians had been so conscious of their intellectual and spiritual superiority, who would ever have invited them to a cocktail party? But the 'Church within the Church' proclaims two important principles that are reflected in the Guardians also — the acceptance of responsibility for the welfare of the souls of others as well as of their own, and the affirmation of a choice that may have to be made in harmony with an inward vocation; one will lead to 'virtue and well-being in community', as in the case of the Chamberlaynes, and the other to 'beatitude', that is, to sainthood, as in the case of Celia Coplestone; they are the two ways of Christian love, neither better than the other, but both necessary, which are the subject of the play,

Seen in this light the question by what right the Guardians take it upon themselves to intervene in the inmost lives of others falls to the ground; they do so not as a *right* but as a *duty*, and try to live the life of a Good Samaritan according to the parable, and not 'pass by on the other side'. In other respects the Guardians do not much resemble 'the Church within the Church', for they are full of fun; but after all, Eliot was ten years wiser when he created them than when he first tried to formulate the nature of a Christian community.

(e) *In the consulting room*

Julia and Alex, Sir Henry's sheep-dogs, have succeeded in driving Edward and Lavinia, the black sheep, and Celia the white, into their several pens in his Consulting Rooms at their prearranged times, and the excitements of psycho-analytical treatment begin with the startling deflation of the Chamberlaynes; it is Edward's turn first to be submitted to the necessary humiliations to puncture his ingrown self-deception; when this process seems complete and he declares he has had enough of it and tries to break off the interview, Sir Henry rings the bell for his Nurse-Secretary who brings in Lavinia, whose turn has come; husband and wife are stunned by this highly unprofessional confrontation — for Group Therapy was not in vogue in 1940. Edward's relationship with Celia is laid bare in front of his wife (who claims to have known it all before) and Lavinia's unrequited attachment to Peter Quilpe is also revealed, to the delight of Edward, who, vain and obtuse, had never imagined such a thing. It is a scene of highest satirical pleasure to listen to Sir Henry's remorseless analysis, which reaches its climax in its demonstration that their situations are so similar as to create a bond between them:

Reilly   And now you begin to see, I hope,
          How much you have in common. The same isolation.
          A man who finds himself incapable of loving
          And a woman who finds that no man can love her.
Lavinia It seems to me that what we have in common
          Might be just enough to make us loathe one another.
Reilly   See it rather as the bond which holds you together.
          While still in a state of unenlightenment,
          You could always say: 'he could not love any woman;'
          You could always say: 'no man could love her.'
          You could accuse each other of your own faults,
          And so could avoid understanding each other.
          Now, you have only to reverse the propositions
          And put them together.

                                                    (II. 378–91)

You could accuse each other of your own faults — and therefore they could punish each other for their own guilts; but now that they have been enlightened, she should see that he might love her if only she were more lovable, and he that she was lovable, if only he could learn to love. It may be that in writing this, Eliot was remembering the ultimate advice given by Nature to the Dreamer, at the end of the B Text of *Piers Plowman*:

   'Conseille me, Kynde,' quod I 'what crafte is best to lerne?'
   'Lerne to love,' quod Kynde, 'and leve of alle othre.'
                                                    (B. XX. 206–7)

   ('Counsel me, Nature,' said I, 'what knowledge is the best to
        learn?'
   'Learn to love', said Nature, 'and leave all other learning.')

Sharp-eyed and practical, Lavinia sees the truth of what Sir Henry has said to them, and she sees the risk in following his advice; to be fair to Sir Henry, he foresees it too:

> what have they to go back to?
> To the stale food mouldering in the larder,
> The stale thoughts mouldering in their minds.
> Each unable to disguise his own meanness
> From himself, because it is known to the other . . .
> I have taken a great risk.
>
> (II. 742–50)

But if it is the way of danger, it is also the way of hope, and Lavinia presses forward to it, not by asserting her will or laying down a course of action, but more subtly, more generously, appealing to Edward, to take command and solve their problem, as if she trusted in him for guidance and strength; she launches her appeal to him over Sir Henry's head, as to a final authority:

> Then what can we do
> When we can go neither back nor forward? Edward!
> What can we do?
>
> (II. 399–401)

and Edward is touched and rises to the occasion, humbly, and yet with a certain grandeur, in another little moment of greatness, notwithstanding the utter mediocrity of his turn of phrase:

> Lavinia, we must make the best of a bad job.
> That is what he means.
>
> (II. 403–4)

It is the first time she has used his Christian name without a sneer, the first time he has used hers with kindly affection. In the first draft this subtle touch was not present; it is one of 'the felicities' of which Martin Browne speaks, in

266

describing Eliot's craftsmanship,* added in production. This tense appeal has brought them to the threshold of a reconciliation and so it is the moment for a return from drama to comedy; Edward, a little ruefully, decides that he had better go home. The ever-practical Lavinia pounces on his decision and clinches it:

> Then we can share a taxi, and be economical.
>
> (II. 420)

It is a touch that would have delighted Congreve.

It is now Celia's turn, and, when the Chamberlaynes have left, she is admitted to the Consulting Room. Her approach to her problems is markedly different from theirs; it is almost as if she belonged to another order of human beings. This beautiful society girl comes in humble and bewildered, 'in desperation' she says (II. 468); she has no one to blame but herself (475) and cannot think her trouble is of any interest to others. When pressed to explain her perplexity, she diffidently speaks of two unusual symptoms that she has experienced. The first is a sense of her *solitude*, not only hers, but the general isolation of all human beings from each other; everyone is profoundly alone. 'They make noises', she says, 'and think they are talking to each other; they make faces and think they understand each other' (II. 529–30).

Yet she is speaking to Sir Henry, and it seems that he understands her well. Her second symptom is more remarkable still; she has a sense of *sin*. By that she does not mean that she feels 'immoral' (in her relations with Edward); she means far more:

> It's not the feeling of anything I've ever *done*,
> Which I might get away from, or of anything in me
> I could get rid of — but of emptiness, of failure
> Towards someone, or something, outside of myself;

> And I feel I must . . . *atone* — is that the word?
> Can you treat a patient for such a state of mind?
>
> (II. 580–5)

Celia has other phrases that hint at her condition; the world she lives in 'seems all a delusion' (486), whereas her sense of sin might prove more real than anything she had believed in (578). And again she says she is like a child who has wandered into a forest playing with an imaginary playmate, who suddenly discovers he is only a child lost in a forest, wanting to go home (607–10).

> But even if I find my way out of the forest
> I shall be left with the inconsolable memory
> Of the treasure I went into the forest to find
> And never found, and which is not there
> And perhaps is not anywhere? But if not anywhere,
> Why do I feel guilty at not having found it?
>
> (II. 613–18)

What are we to make of these hints and imageries? She says also that she thinks she has had a vision, but of what she cannot say; but it is a vision which above all things she would wish to cherish and live with, that demands a kind of love that she could give to no one else:

> I couldn't give anyone the kind of love —
> I wish I could — which belongs to that life.
>
> (II. 669–70)

These are among the stirrings of her conversion, whose compelling purposes are as yet unclear to her, yet she feels her way towards them poetically, as we might expect of her, since we have been told she is a poet (I. 1. 465). Her intuition tells her of a treasure in a forest sought for in vain, yet so precious as to leave her inconsolable in its loss; yet it must happen somewhere, this 'infinite felicity', if we may borrow Madame Odintsov's phrase.

These insights have much in common with those of Harry in *The Family Reunion*, though his sense of sin is more violent than hers and his search for expiation cruder; love is what marks the great advance which *The Cocktail Party* makes over *The Family Reunion*, in its account of a religious conversion. Harry, of course, is a wilder, unhappier figure than Celia; he believes himself to have murdered his wife. Celia is gentler and wiser, and she is capable of a life:

> In which one is exalted by intensity of loving
> In the spirit, a vibration of delight
> Without desire, for desire is fulfilled
> In the delight of loving . . .
> > . . . But what, or whom I loved,
> Or what in me was loving, I do not know.

> (II. 626–31)

Yet Celia is unsure whether this vision of hers is false or meaningless, and if so, whether she can be cured of 'the shame of never finding it' (II. 634).

Sir Henry confirms her intuitions; there is another kind of life, based upon faith, he says:

> The kind of faith that issues from despair.
> The destination cannot be described;
> You will know very little until you get there;
> You will journey blind. But the way leads towards possession
> Of what you have sought for in the wrong place.

> (II. 679–83)

He shows her that she must choose between this dangerous way and the way of common humanity, 'the human condition' of ordinary love in marriage:

> with the morning that separates
> And with the evening that brings together
> For casual talk before the fire

Two people who know they do not understand each other,
Breeding children whom they do not understand
And who will never understand them.

(II. 647–52)

Celia chooses the unknown and more dangerous way and, in doing so, passes beyond the point at which Sir Henry can help her, except by sending her to his special sanatorium, that is, to a religious Order, where she will be trained to fulfil her austere vocation. After her departure, Julia enters by a side door, and presently she and Sir Henry are joined by Alex. For the first time we see the three Guardians alone together.

(f) *The Libation*

They have met to pray for those they have guarded and guided: for the Chamberlaynes in their homely but home-creating task of making a real marriage out of their empty union, and for Celia on her austere journey into the unknown dangers of a mystical vocation. It was to be a little ceremony of prayer which they called '*a Libation*', because it included a pouring out of wine in a kind of drink-offering. It could suggest a classic ritual for those to whom a Christian prayer might cause offence or embarrassment, and at the same time symbolise a sacramental act for those whose imaginations were of a Christian cast. The form the Libation takes more nearly resembles a toast over a glass of sherry and this ingeniously keeps in sight the cocktail party element in the play, while turning it to a more serious, ritual use.

In making so daring an experiment in drawing-room comedy, Eliot faced a major self-contradiction in the strategy he had chosen for offering Christian plays to agnostic audiences; he had denied himself the open preaching of a Christian sermon, for he had already said his say by way of sermons in the choruses of *The Rock* and in *Murder in the Cathedral* — Christian sermons addressed to Christian audiences. But now he had adopted a technique of symbolism, a form of poetic imagination that he had learnt from France in earlier years. So in *The Family Reunion* he had used 'the imagery of the Eumenides to suggest how a soul, convinced of sin, could be first hounded, but at last guided, by the angels of conscience, towards expiation, through a better understanding of love and sacrifice; he had achieved this, however, at the cost of deep obscurity. Yet it had permitted him to indulge his feeling for liturgy or ceremonial of a quasi-religious kind, by concluding the play with a magical incantation and a processional blowing-out of candles.

The Libation scene in *The Cocktail Party* attempts a comparable effect. It was essential to bring the second Act to a climax which should declare the religious character of the Guardians in a corporate action, that would gather the purposes of the play together and speed it along towards its spiritual goal. It should be a climax that would crown all that has gone before, and, at the same time, engender feelings of surprise and suspense, on which to launch the last Act.

Up till this point in the play, Eliot had succeeded in avoiding all mention of Christianity; it is true that 'the saints' had been spoken of (II. 406), but there are saints in other religions; there are even agnostic saints. Now, however, intent upon the religious ritual which his love of classical Greek had taught him to think of as an essential of drama, he was faced with the task of writing a prayer for one about to become a Christian martyr, to be spoken by those who, though not apparently Christian themselves, had helped to send her to her martyrdom. Were they in fact Christians? Should their prayers be Christian prayers, or conceived in some elevated pagan style suited to their 'intellectual superiority'? Or should they be neutral, non-committal?

Had it been Eliot's intention to write an openly Christian play, or a play to illustrate his *Idea of a Christian Society*, the natural thing would have been for the Guardians, at least when alone with each other, to confess their Christianity and kneel down to offer up a Christian prayer; but naturalism is not everything, even in a drawing-room comedy; what was needed at the end of a long and serious Act was a sudden bright surprise, in keeping with the Guardian character of unpredictable levity blended with high seriousness — the gesture of a toast, the language of a prayer.

Eliot found a model for such a language in a work by Dr. Alexander Carmichael called *Carmina Gadelica*, that began to be published in a series of volumes in 1900. They consisted of 'hymns and incantations . . . orally collected in the Highlands and Islands of Scotland'. A more recent volume, comprising the first four volumes of Carmichael's collection, with additions, was published under the title *Poems from the Western Highlanders* (1961), from the Gaelic, by G. R. D. McLean. Examples taken from this work show how it kindled Eliot's imagination:

> I have over thee the power of the silver moon,
> I have over thee the power of the fierce sun,
> I have over thee the power of the rain's wet shoon,
> I have over thee the power of the dew spun . . .
>
> Be with us through the time of each day,
> Be with us through the time of each night . . .
>
> White-beamed Father, Son, Holy Spirit bright,
> Be the Three-in-One with us day and night,

On the sandy plain, on the hill-ridge led,
Three-in-One with us, guide-hand in our head,
Three-in-One our helmet-hand round the head.

In his original draft Eliot indulged his fantasy; indeed, he *over*-indulged it with a mixture of symbols which he later repented and ruled out; they read more like mystification than mysticism (see Martin Browne, op. cit., p. 187):

Alex The prayer for the building of the hearth:
Let them build the hearth
Under the protection of the Moon,
And place a chair on each side of it.
Who shall surround the house?
J and R The four higher protectors.
Alex Who shall watch over the roof?
J and R The two winged ones shall watch over the roof.
Alex Under what sign shall it be erected?
J and R Under the sign of the seven stars.
Alex Who shall cast influence upon the bed?
J and R The Moon shall influence the bed.
Alex In what name shall she act?
J and R In the name of the fructifying Sun.

Rational thought, rejecting the intrusion of things symbolic, might pause here prosily to ask whether so eminent a scientist as Sir Henry Harcourt-Reilly really believed that the sun, moon and stars could hear and grant his prayers, or whether it was a piece of mumbo-jumbo for theatrical effect; and there might be further questions: Who were 'the four higher protectors'? Could they be Matthew, Mark, Luke and John? Were the 'two winged ones' over the roof (changed later to 'two holy ones') a cherub and a seraph? Or a reminiscence of a famous Botticelli Nativity in the National Gallery, in which angels dance on the roof of the Bethlehem manger?

Eliot has removed the necessity of answering these questions by removing 'the higher protectors' and 'the winged ones' from his final text, leaving us with the simpler symbolism of Nature-Worship (sun, moon and stars) to do duty for a Christian acknowledgement of:

> the Name which is not spoken,

to use the phrase which concluded the prayer in its earlier draft, but which was later cancelled, perhaps for consistency. These cancellations are more than made up for in the final version by a last twist of wit; the draft had ended thus:

R   But there is one for whom we do nothing.
J   It is Peter whom he means.
A   Peter? What Peter?
R   The young man Peter Quilpe.
A   There are things beyond our powers
      Which must be left to the mystery and the mercy.

Fortunately these lines were dropped; in their stead Eliot wrote:

R   There is one for whom the words cannot be spoken.
A   They cannot be spoken yet.
J   You mean Peter Quilpe.
R   He has not yet come to where the words are valid.
J   Shall we ever speak them?
A   Others, perhaps, will speak them.
      You know, I have connections — even in California.
                         (II. 809–13)

The idea that by the time Peter Quilpe needs spiritual guidance there may be a Christian society, even in California, brings down the curtain with a run.

It is hard to assess what Eliot has achieved in this astonishing second Act. It creates and sustains an absorbed attention or empathy; every word of the pyschoanalysis sharpens excitement: the Libation is a startling, last-moment surprise: it is serious and it is comic: Eliot has kept to his strategy: he has kept to his love of ritual and symbolism: he has kept the excitement alive to the last instant: he has created a kind of cliff-hanger suspense, to lead us to the heart of the last Act: above all he has kept his secret — the Christian cat is still safely in the seemingly pagan bag, ready for the stunning effect when it is to spring out with the news of Celia's crucifixion, brought by Alex from far Kinkanja.

(g) *The fulfilments of love*

Two years have passed and the intensity of the Consulting Room now gives way to the frivolity of the Chamberlayne flat. The Chamberlaynes are about to give another cocktail party. Lavinia gives her final orders to the caterer's man as her husband returns from a day's work in his chambers. The audience settles itself pleasurably for the business of the last Act, which can be no other than to satisfy its curiosity about the success or failure of Sir Henry's psychotherapy.

The Chamberlaynes are certainly on friendly terms, for they chaff each other on the very subject that might be expected to produce explosions; Lavinia says:

> . . . all I rang up for was to reassure you . . .
> *Edward* (smiling) That you hadn't run away?
> *Lavinia* Now Edward, that's unfair!
>> You know that we've given *several* parties
>> In the last two years. And I've attended *all* of them.
>> (III. 12–15)

A gay but humdrum conversation flows along, suggesting their unity, even their amity — a little too strongly, perhaps; the embarrassing suspicion arises in our minds that they are being *too* kind to each other, or, worse still, '*polite*', in their mutual solicitude: we hear phrases liike 'I hope you're not too tired' . . . 'It's you who should be tired' . . . 'I like the dress you're wearing' which set a satirical mind wondering how long a marriage could last on mere good manners and soft sugar. However the question is swiftly swept aside by the imperious doorbell rung (of course) by Julia, who has brought Alex with her.

Where has he come from? From Kinkanja! And with a globe-trotter's enthusiasm he launches into a ludicrous account of the monkey-problem in that remote and little-known region. We are back in the mood of high comedy that started the play off so amusingly with talk of tigers and Maharajahs, and which is now extended to Sultans and monkeys, heathens and Christians. The heathens revere the monkeys, the Christian converts eat them; Alex has not only cooked and eaten them himself, but has invented several new recipes for the natives.

As the talk butterflies its way along among these topics, the mood is suddenly, for an instant, changed by Alex, taking up his cue from Lavinia:

> Ah, the Christians! Now I think I ought to tell you
> About someone you know — or knew . . .

> (III. 174–5)

Julia knows the news he is about to deliver; it is about Celia, and she breaks in to delay it until those who should hear it have all gathered in the Chamberlaynes' flat. 'Edward' she says, 'Somebody must have walked over my grave . . . Give me some gin.' It is a subtle warning, the creation of a *frisson* of suspense tinged with anxiety, and produces a presentiment, vague as yet, but chilling. The effect, however, is almost instantly dispelled by the arrival of .Peter Quilpe. We are not told whether Julia or Alex knew he would be joining the party once more, but it may be guessed that she did, since Peter had told Sheila Paisley that he was going to call on the Chamberlaynes (III. 186) and she may well have passed the news on to Julia, ever in the thick of things social.

Peter has just flown in from New York, full of his own doings, and by one of those coincidences that so often happen in life — far more often than they are allowed to happen in literature — he tells them of a newly fashionable restaurant where he had dined a few nights before:

> We dined the other night
> At the Saffron Monkey. That's the place to go now.
>
> (III. 196–7)

'How very odd!' comments Alex, '*My* monkeys are saffron.' The subject of the Kinkanja monkeys is once again about to be developed, but once again Julia fends it off; we may assume she is secretly waiting for the arrival of Sir Henry Harcourt-Reilly before allowing Alex to give his news. Is it because she knows he is the only one among them who is of sufficient stature in understanding to expound the inward truth of Celia's martyrdom, and what we should think of it?

At last Sir Henry enters; the whole company has thus assembled once more in the Chamberlaynes' flat, all except one. Where is Celia?

The question is put by Peter Quilpe; he wants to cast her for his next film, but he cannot find her name in the telephone directory. Julia says:

> Not in the directory,
> Or in any directory. You can tell them now, Alex.
>
> (III. 299–300)

Alex tells them that Celia is dead. In telling them that she died in Kinkanja, and how she died, we see the sudden relevance of the monkeys, worshipped by the heathen there. An insurrection had broken out among the heathen against the Christians. Celia, nursing the natives in a Christian village, where they were dying of war and pestilence, had been taken prisoner:

> When our people got there, they questioned the villagers —
> Those who survived. And then they found her body,
> Or at least, they found the traces of it.
>
> (III. 327–9)

> . . . from what we know of local practices
> It would seem that she must have been crucified
> Very near an ant-hill.
>
> (III. 331–3)

Those who reject this climax as too horrible for comedy have missed the point of the play, one of the purposes of which, as we have seen, is to show a saint and martyr in the making and the kind of love demanded of a saint. This is a perspective that is not commonly shown in comedies, or in drawing-rooms either, and it falls to Sir Henry to tell his hearers how they should think of the news that has so briefly and so brutally been delivered.

It is a perspective long since explained by Eliot through the mouth of St. Thomas of Canterbury in *Murder in the Cathedral*, a play which is the tragic Christian pillar that supports so much of what is in this secular comedy. In the sermon at the centre of this play, St. Thomas tells us how to think of martyrdom:

> Beloved, we do not think of a martyr simply as a good Christian who has been killed because he is a Christian: for that would be solely to mourn. We do not think of him simply as a good Christian who has been elevated to the company of the Saints: for that would be simply to rejoice: and neither our mourning nor our rejoicing is as the

world's is. A Christian martyrdom is never an accident,
for Saints are not made by accident . . . A martyrdom is
always the design of God . . . for the true martyr is he who
has become the instrument of God . . . and who no longer
desires anything for himself, not even the glory of being
a martyr. So thus as on earth the Church mourns and
rejoices at once, in a fashion that the world cannot understand.

This vision of heroic sanctity, seen by Eliot in the martyrdom of St. Thomas of Canterbury in the twelfth century,
was equally seen by him in that of Celia Coplestone in the
twentieth. How was he to expound it, in its inevitability, its
terror and its glory, above all, perhaps, in its mystery, in a
London drawing-room?

There was only one among his characters of a sufficient
spiritual stature to speak of such things — Sir Henry
Harcourt-Reilly; yet even he and his finely phrased, conversational habit of speech, would not sound very plausible
if he were suddenly to rise, on his own, to great intensities of
poetic language. Yet great intensities were needed of him.
Eliot hit on an expedient of the greatest ingenuity. He
would make Sir Henry quote Shelley. Sir Henry would
know his Shelley, Shelley would supply the intensity.

He found the passage he needed already quoted in a novel
called *Descent into Hell* by Charles Williams, a close friend of
his. It had recently been published in 1937. The passage
came from the first Act of *Prometheus Unbound* and described the eerie experience of meeting with one's double:

> Ere Babylon was dust
> The magus Zoroaster, my dead child,
> Met his own image walking in the garden.
> That apparition, sole of men, he saw.

(III. 423–6)

There was no reason to suppose that Sir Henry would be

incapable of quoting Shelley; there was equally no reason why sir Henry might not be endowed with the strange gift of Second Sight, upon occasion. It is a well-attested phenomenon ever among the hardest-headed. Eliot settled for this way of solving his problem. Sir Henry (after asking permission from Lavinia, the least poetical person present) preludes his story with ten of Shelley's eeriest lines, to prepare them for his strange experience:

> When I first met Miss Coplestone, in this room,
> I saw the image, standing behind her chair,
> Of a Celia Coplestone whose face showed the astonishment
> Of the first five minutes after a violent death.
> If this strains your credulity, Mrs. Chamberlayne,
> I ask you only to entertain the suggestion
> That a sudden intuition, in certain minds,
> May tend to express itself at once in a picture.
> That happens to me, sometimes. So it was obvious
> That here was a woman under sentence of death.

(III. 432–41)

That Celia's death could be thus 'foreseen' suggests the presence of the 'design' that St. Thomas speaks of, a design to which Celia, by the surrender of her will and power of loving into the will and love of God, has freely consented. Reilly also refers to this 'design'; in speaking of what Celia suffered in the way of pain, compared with what ordinary people, not martyrs or ecstatics, might suffer, he says:

> She paid the highest price
> In suffering. That is part of the design.

(III. 460)

For some approach to a definition of this mystical 'design' as Eliot saw it, we may again turn to *Murder in the Cathedral*:

> . . . action is suffering
> And suffering is action. Neither does the agent suffer

Nor the patient act. Both are fixed
In an eternal action, an eternal patience
To which all must consent that it may be willed
And which all must suffer that they may will it,
That the pattern may subsist, for the pattern is the action
And the suffering, that the wheel may turn and still
Be forever still.

(Part I, 209–17)

It is the pattern set by the Incarnation and Crucifixion of Christ. Celia has willingly filled in her part in the pattern; so Reilly can declare her death to have been triumphant.

Celia has found, in her way of life and death, the fulfilment of her power to love, '*to suffren love's hete celestial*'. As Sir Henry says:

That way, which she accepted, led to this death.
And if that is not a happy death, what death is happy?

(III. 450–1)

The little party breaks up; Peter leaves for California; Julia collects her fellow Guardians and sweeps them imperiously off to another party and the Chamberlaynes are left alone, awaiting the guests they have invited; they are still in the same idyllic mood in which the scene started; Lavinia fishes, Edward dotes:

Lavinia Edward, how am I looking?
Edward   Very well.
        I might almost say, your best. But you always look your best.

(III. 548–9)

The explanation of Edward's extreme solicitude, his flattering tenderness, is given in Eliot's letter to Sir Geoffrey Faber (see p. 192 f.). Lavinia is going to have a baby. This is the fulfilment of the love of kynde.

281

(h) *Influences and sources*

We should distinguish between influences and sources in considering the conceptions on which *The Cocktail Party* is based. Its sources are those works from which specific passages are directly and identifiably taken and used, or imitated, in Eliot's play; there are four of these. There is first the ballad of *One-Eyed Riley*, the work of the anonymous popular Muse, from which Eliot took a verse and chorus to supply Sir Henry with a necessary music-hall song. It is necessary because of what happens in the second source, to which Eliot confessed with glee in his well-known Harvard lecture on 'Poetry and Drama', given in 1950. His debt in *The Cocktail Party*, he told his astonished hearers, was to the *Alcestis* of Euripides:

> I was still inclined to go to a Greek dramatist for my theme, but I was determined to do so merely as a point of departure, and to conceal the origins so well that nobody would identify them until I pointed them out myself. In this last I have been successful; for no one of my acquaintance (and no dramatic critics) recognised the source of my story in the *Alcestis* of Euripides. In fact I have had to go into detailed explanation to convince them — I mean, of course, those who were familiar with the plot of that play — of the genuineness of the inspiration. But those who were at first disturbed by the eccentric behaviour of my unknown guest, and his apparently intemperate habits and tendency to burst into song, have found some consolation after I have called their attention to the behaviour of Heracles in Euripides' play.

Alcestis was the wife of Admetus, who had put the god Apollo under an obligation. To discharge his obligation, Apollo cheated the Fates into allowing Admetus to escape death, if he could find anyone willing to take his place and die instead of him. Admetus tried to persuade his father and mother to do him this service, but he had no success with them. His wife, Alcestis, however freely offered to take his place and die that he might live, and the play opens with the news that she is at the point of death already, and the whole house is in mourning for her impending doom.

At this moment Heracles, an old friend of Admetus, unexpectedly arrives, on the way to perform his Eighth Labour (the capture of the man-eating horses of Diomedes) and is hospitably received by Admetus, who conceals from him the cause of the general grief, inviting him in and offering him a feast, so as not to seem inhospitable. Heracles enters, is lavishly provided for, and takes full advantage of what is set before him and more. By the time Alcestis is borne off lifeless to her tomb, Heracles is so drunk as to scandalise the servants, one of whom enters to tell the audience all about it:

> 'He refused to understand the situation and be content with anything we could provide, but when we failed to bring him something, demanded it, and took a cup with ivy on it in both hands and drank the wine of our dark mother, straight until the flame of the wine went all through him, and heated him, and then he wreathed branches of myrtle on his head and howled off key. There were two kinds of music now to hear, for while he sang and never gave a thought to the sorrows of Admetus, we servants were mourning for our mistress . . .'*

Heracles then returns to the scene, drunk but not incapable, and by cross-examining the servant learns the truth about Alcestis. He determines at once to save her by watching for 'Death of the Black Robes', whom he means to hold in the circle of his huge arms until he gives the woman up to him. It need hardly be said that in the Euripedean version of this myth, the drunken demi-god is successful and brings Alcestis safely back to the arms of her husband. In like manner the One-Eyed Riley arrives on the very afternoon of Lavinia's desertion of Edward, drinks a lot of gin and water, at Edward's expense, promises to bring her back within twenty-four hours, and makes his exit singing a lewd song, 'howled off-key'.

Verbal touches of poetic reminder give things, slender enough to elude the source-seeker, but strong enough to be triumphantly pointed out by the author, when all the critics had failed; for instance, Sir Henry says:

> it is a serious matter
> *To bring someone back from the dead.*
>
> *Edward*   *From the dead?*
> That figure of speech is somewhat . . . dramatic,
> As it was only yesterday my wife left me.
> *Unidentified Guest*   Ah, but we die to each other daily.
>
> (I. 3. 20–23 My italics)

Another hint to tease non-Euripideans with comes later in the play, when Lavinia has been brought back from her 'sanatorium', and is talking, for once with some tenderness, to her husband of their broken marriage:

> I thought there might be some way out for you
> If I went away. *I thought that if I died*
> *To you*, I who had only been a ghost to you,
> You might be able to find the road back
> To a time when you were real. . . .
>
> (I. 3. 399–403 My italics)

Sources can be demonstrated; they leave their finger-prints. Influences permeate but are less specific. I have already mentioned the pervading influences of Shakespeare and of the Comedy of Manners; but there are others also, at a greater depth, traceable to the excitement of those early discoveries in anthropology made famous by Sir James

Fraser's *Golden Bough* (1890–1915), which started many trains of thought at the time; one of them was embodied in a work by F. M. Cornford, called *The Origin of Attic Comedy* (1914, republished in 1934) to which Eliot confessed he was deeply indebted for its insistence on ritual significance in drama.* In this book Cornford contended that the comedies of Aristophanes contained a ritual of a Dionysiac or phallic kind; they invariably included a Sacrifice, a Feast, a Marriage and a Phallic Procession. We are shown Sacrifice in Celia, Marriage in Edward and Lavinia, whose pregnancy represents the phallic element; the Feast is treated as a joke; it is the 'toothsome morsel' concocted by Alexander MacColgie Gibbs for the distracted Edward, and which is burnt to a cinder.

This is an Aristophanic joke that Eliot has used once before, in the second fragment of *Sweeney Agonistes*; we have Eliot's authority for saying that when the fragment is performed, Sweeney should be cooking a dish of eggs;* an egg is of course a symbol of life at its most elementary and primitive; as Sweeney says:

> You see this egg
> You see this egg
> Well that's life on a crocodile isle.

MacColgie Gibbs is the comic cook, preparing the ritual meal.

These are the esoteric significances or creative allusions that are semi-secretly mixed in with other elements that go to make *The Cocktail Party*, for the pleasure of those who can detect and appreciate them, and perhaps for the even greater pleasure of the author when they are *not* detected.

(i) *'Poetry' and verse*

The dialogue of *The Cocktail Party*, as of all Eliot's plays, is printed in lines of verse, to help the reader or actor to speak them properly by indicating their intended rhythms; they suggest pauses and stresses and breath lengths, singling out words of special importance; for instance, a reader confronted by the following sentence:

> You and I don't know the process by which the human is transhumanised: what do we know of the kind of suffering they must undergo on the way of illumination?

might well miss the infinitesimal pauses and stresses of:

> You and I don't know the process by which the human is/
> *Transhumanised*: what do *we* know
> Of the kind of suffering *they* must undergo/
> On the way to illumination?

(II. 766–9)

The unusual word *transhumanised* is picked out by a kind of hesitation at the end of the line, before the speaker 'finds' it, and a similar pause is placed after *undergo*, to make the contrast between *suffering* and *illumination*: this draws our attention to the further contrast between *we* and *they*. I have supplied clumsy italics and bar-lines to emphasise the nuances of the text that Eliot has indicated by writing the speech in verses. This method of helping an actor is more necessary in *The Family Reunion*, where there are far greater obscurities of thought than in *The Cocktail Party*. Indeed, the latter is a play as lucid as any play of Shaw, the great master of lucidity in prose dialogue.

That the lines are written in verses does not mean that they are staking a claim to be considered as 'poetry'. Nor is it useful to describe them as 'prose cut up into lengths'. They are cut up into *rhythms* that have meaning; each line asks for the kind of attention which it specially deserves as a component in the general meaning of the passage in which it comes, and in the general effect of human talk, with its irregular stresses and pauses. Yet human talk has its moments of poetry, which Eliot has ever been careful to capture; he shows a rare ear for natural idiom and how to make it tell in a poem; one has only to read *The Love Song of J. Alfred Prufrock*, *The Waste Land* (especially the rejected passages now made available to us by Mrs. Eliot's splendid edition) and *Sweeney Agonistes*, to perceive his extraordinary gift in this art of talk, that so deftly intensifies his effects. That intensity rather than metre is the true source of poetry is claimed by him in a lecture on 'The Three Voices of Poetry', given in 1953 to the National Book League:

> In a verse play, you will probably have to find words for several characters differing widely from each other in background, temperament, education and intelligence. You cannot afford to identify one of these characters with yourself, and give him or her all the 'poetry' to speak. The poetry (*I mean the language at those dramatic moments when it reaches intensity*) must be as widely distributed as characterisation permits; and each of your characters, when he has words to speak which are poetry and not merely verse, must be given lines appropriate to himself.

I have italicised the essential idea, that poetry is language used with intensity, and I would like to contrast this account of its nature with a famous definition offered by S. T. Coleridge in his *Table Talk* (12 July 1827):

> I wish our clever young poets would remember my homely definitions of prose and poetry; that is, prose equals words in their best order; — poetry equals the *best* words in the best order.

It is evident that to substitute 'intensity' for 'goodness' is a great step forward from Coleridge; one can think of many sentences superlatively well-expressed that are still not what we mean by 'poetry'; for instance '*Two and two are four.*' These are certainly the best words in the best order for the particular notion they express, but they would be judged by most people to be purest prose, in spite of A. E. Housman's rueful quatrain:

> To think that two and two are four,
>   And neither five nor three,
> The heart of man has long been sore,
>   And long is like to be.

When Eliot began on his great work of restoring poetry to our stage, he tried to find or fashion a language that achieved an intensity of rhythm, as well as of imagery. Of this achievement he wrote later (in his Theodore Spencer Memorial Lecture, 1950):

> As for the versification, I was only aware at this stage that the essential was to avoid any echo of Shakespeare. . . . The rhythm of regular blank verse had become too remote from the movement of modern speech. Therefore what I kept in mind was the versification of *Everyman*.

This revolutionary versification, which was based on 'an avoidance of too much iambic', continued to develop towards an increasingly conversational movement and tone, adhering, but not slavishly, to the rules he tells us he formulated for himself:

> What I worked out is substantially what I have continued to employ: a line of varying length and varying number of syllables, with a caesura and three stresses. The caesura and the stresses may come at different places almost anywhere in the line; the stresses may be close together or well separated by light syllables, the only rule being that there must be one stress on one side of the caesura and two on the other.

He came even to relaxing his avoidance of iambic move-
ment and of admitting brief intrusions of blank verse itself.
Many such intrusions will be found in *The Cocktail Party*.
For instance:

> There *is* another way, if you have the courage.
> The first I could describe in familiar terms
> * Because you have seen it, as we all have seen it,
> Illustrated, more or less, in lives of those about us.
> The second is unknown, and so requires faith —
> * The kind of faith that issues from despair.
> * The destination cannot be described.

(II. 674–80)

I have marked with an asterisk three normal blank-verse
lines, and might include a fourth by a slight elision, thus:

> There is another way if you've the courage.

The caesuras fall after way/ describe/ seen it/ or less/
unknown/. There is no caesura in either of the last two
lines, no hint of pause; the last but one has four lightish
stresses:

> The *kind* of *faith* that *iss*ues from des*pair*

and the last has but three:

> The *dest*ination *can*not be des*cribed*

This is traditional blank verse usage; compare:

> The *qual*ity of *mer*cy is not *strained* (3)
> It *drop*peth as the *gent*le *rain* from *heaven* (4)
> > (*The Merchant of Venice*, IV. 183–4)

or

> But *see* the *ang*ry *Vic*tor hath *recalled* (4)
> His *Min*isters of *veng*eance and pur*suit* (3)
> > (*Paradise Lost*, I. 169–70)

Perhaps Eliot's most ingenious use of blank verse in *The Cocktail Party* is in the mouth of Sir Henry Harcourt-Reilly, when he seeks to pierce Lavinia's boasted practicality with a touch of poetry, by quoting the mysterious passage from Shelley's *Prometheus Unbound* (III. 423–31). It creates a sudden escalation of intensity which may be due as much to its majestic regularity of iambic movement as to the strangeness of the experience it describes. It is in a language beyond the reach of conversation.

To sum up: in *The Cocktail Party*, each line, as printed, has its own autonomous length and rhythm as a sentence, or part of a sentence, lightly indicating how it is to be spoken, where the emphasis should fall, and where the pauses (if any) are to come, if the meaning is to be fully expressed, and the quality of conversation is to be preserved. The 'poetry' (that is, the intensity) flows through the lines with varying strength, related to the situation and the character of the speaker.

Lines are sometimes broken up between two speakers. I have no warrant for saying so, but I think that when this happens, the broken pieces are meant to take each other up in brief interchange. For instance:

> *Celia*   That's all that matters. Truly, Edward,
> If that is right, everything else will be,
> I promise you.
> *Edward*   No, Celia.
> It has been very wonderful, and I'm very grateful,
> And I think you are a very rare person.
> But it is too late. And I should have known
> That it wasn't fair to you.
> *Celia*   It wasn't fair to *me*!
> You can stand there and talk about being fair to *me*!
>   (I. 2. 157–64)

Here 'No Celia' belongs to the sequence of meaning that

culminates in 'I promise you'; but 'It has been very wonderful' starts a new idea — Edward's gauche effort to pat Celia
on the back; if the lines had been printed thus:

> *Celia*   If that is right, everything else will be,
>   I promise you.
> *Edward* No, Celia. It has been very wonderful
>   And I'm very grateful, and I think
>   You are a very rare person.

Edward's refusal would seem a more settled, a more
deliberate choice. Similarly Celia's repetition of Edward's
phrase:

> it wasn't fair to you.
>   It wasn't fair to *me*!

belongs to her anger at this notion, rather than to her
amazement (which is her next emotion) given a line to
itself:

> You can stand there and talk about being fair to *me*!

No doubt her amazement has some anger in it still, but it is
amazement that predominates in the repetition, to my ear,
at least. Typography does not make poetry, but it may help
the speaker to recognise and speak it. There is no new
doctrine as to the nature of poetry in relation to verse or
even to prose, in *The Cocktail Party*. There is simply the
culmination of a long search for a way of writing that would
admit the intensity of poetry without losing the flavour of
conversation. When for a moment Eliot needs something of
even greater intensity, he abandons conversation and turns
to Shelley.

5   Notes to the Essay

5 Notes to the Essay

Page 239
Congreve and Shakespeare. Compare John Lawlor, 'The Formal Achievement of *The Cocktail Party*', *Virginia Quarterly Review*, Vol. 30, 1954, pp. 431–51.

Page 242
The Rock, *Murder in the Cathedral* and *The Family Reunion*. For an elaboration of this statement, see my Introduction to the Educational Edition of *The Family Reunion*, Faber, 1969, pp. 11–64.

Page 253
Fathers and Sons by Ivan Turgenev, translated by C. J. Hogarth, Everyman Edition, 1921, Chapter 18.

Page 257
See Martin Browne, *The Making of T. S. Eliot's Plays*, Cambridge University Press, 1969, p. 173. An indispensable book for students of Eliot's drama.

Page 262
The Idea of a Christian Society. This was first noted as a parallel reflection of Eliot's opinion by David E. Jones, in *The Plays of T. S. Eliot*, Routledge & Kegan Paul, 1960, p. 123. The observation is confirmed by Martin Browne, op. cit., p. 185.

Page 267
One of the felicities. Martin Browne, op. cit., p. 212.

Page 283
This quotation is taken from the translation by Richmond Lattimore in *The Complete Greek Tragedies*, edited by

NOTES TO THE ESSAY

David Grene and Richmond Lattimore, University of Chicago Press, 1955.

Page 285

See Eliot's letter to Hallie Flanagan, printed in her book, *Dynamo*, New York, 1943. She had directed his *Sweeney Agonistes* at Vassar in 1933, and had written to Eliot for elucidation of certain points; he replied explaining the importance, in the second fragment of the play, of the ritual cooking of eggs in accordance with Aristophanic precedence.

Page 285

A dish of eggs. See previous note.

6   List of Dates

6 List of Dates

1888   Thomas Stearns Eliot born in St. Louis, U.S.A.

1910   A.B. and A.M. at Harvard University; and studied later at the University of Paris and Merton College, Oxford.

1911   *The Love Song of J. Alfred Prufrock* written.

1915   *The Love Song of J. Alfred Prufrock* published in *Poetry*, 1915.
        Married Vivienne Haigh Haigh-Wood.
        Taught at High Wycombe Grammar School and Highgate School.

1917   Entered the foreign department of Lloyds Bank in the City of London.

1922   Founded and edited *The Criterion* until 1939, in which he published *The Waste Land* in October 1922.

1925   Published *The Hollow Men*.
        Joined Messrs Faber & Gwyer, reconstituted as Faber & Faber in 1929.

1926–7 Published *Sweeney Agonistes* in *The Criterion*.

1927   Became a naturalised British subject; was confirmed into the Church of England.

1934   Wrote *The Rock* from a scenario suggested by the Rev. Webb-Odell and composed by E. Martin Browne, a pageant-play, performed at Sadler's Wells Theatre in May–June.

1935   *Murder in the Cathedral* written for the Canter-
        bury Festival and produced there in June.

1939   Published *The Idea of a Christian Society*.
        Published *The Family Reunion*, which opened at
        the Westminster Theatre in March.

1944   Published the *Four Quartets*.

1948   Published *Notes Towards the Definition of Culture*.
        Awarded the Nobel Prize for Literature.
        Awarded the Order of Merit.

1949   *The Cocktail Party* produced at the Royal
        Lyceum Theatre during the Edinburgh Inter-
        national Festival.

1953   *The Confidential Clerk* produced at the Royal
        Lyceum Theatre during the Edinburgh Inter-
        national Festival; published the following year.

1957   Married Esmé Valerie Fletcher.

1958   *The Elder Statesman* produced during the Edin-
        burgh International Festival; published the
        following year.

1965   Eliot died on 4 January.

7 Selected Reading List

7 Selected Reading List

T. S. Eliot

POETRY

The Waste Land (1923) (See also a facsimile and transcript of the original drafts including the annotations of Ezra Pound, edited by Valerie Eliot, 1971)

Old Possum's Book of Practical Cats (1939)

Four Quartets (1944)

Collected Poems 1909–1962 (1963)

Poems Written in Early Youth (1967)

DRAMA

The Rock (1934)

Murder in the Cathedral (1935) (Educational edition with an introduction and notes by Nevill Coghill, 1965)

The Family Reunion (1939) (Educational edition with an introduction and notes by Nevill Coghill, 1965)

The Elder Statesman (1959)

CRITICISM

The Sacred Wood (1920)

The Idea of a Christian Society (1939)

Selected Essays (1951)

Poetry and Drama (1951)

The Three Voices of Poetry (1953)

Browne, E. Martin *The Making of T. S. Eliot's Plays* (1969) (This work is indispensable to a study of Eliot's development as a practical poet and dramatist.)

Gallup, Donald *T. S. Eliot: A Bibliography* (1969)

SELECTED READING LIST

Gardner, Dame Helen *The Art of T. S. Eliot* (1949)
  'The Comedies of T. S. Eliot' (in *Essays by Diverse Hands*,
  New Series, Royal Society of Literature, Vol. 34, 1964)

Howarth, Herbert *Notes on Some Figures behind T. S. Eliot*
  (1965)

Jones, David E. *The Plays of T. S. Eliot* (1960)

Kojecky, Roger *T. S. Eliot's Social Criticism* (1971)

Lawlor, John 'The Formal Achievement of *The Cocktail
  Party*' (in *Virginia Quarterly Review*, Vol. 30, 1954)

March, Richard and Tambimuttu (eds.) *T. S. Eliot: A Sym-
  posium* (1948)

Matthiessen, F. O. *The Achievement of T. S. Eliot* (3rd
  edition 1958)

Smith, Carol H. *T. S. Eliot's Dramatic Theory and Practice*
  (1963)

Smith, Grover *T. S. Eliot's Poetry and Plays* (1956)

Unger, L. *T. S. Eliot: A Selected Critique* (1948)
  The Man in the Name (1956)

Williamson, G. A. *A Reader's Guide to T. S. Eliot* (1953)